Witches &

in the 21ˢᵗ Century

Katie Boyd

Schiffer
Publishing Ltd

4880 Lower Valley Road, Atglen, Pennsylvania 19310

Other Books by Katie Boyd:

Ghost Quest in New Hampshire   ISBN 978-0-7643-2886-2 $14.95

Rhode Island's Spooky Ghosts and Creepy Legends   ISBN 978-0-7643-3388-0 $14.99

Devils and Demonology in the 21st Century   ISBN 978-0-7643-3195-4 $14.99

Haunted Closets   ISBN 978-0-7643-34-74-0 $14.99

Schiffer Books are available at special discounts for bulk purchases for sales promotions or premiums. Special editions, including personalized covers, corporate imprints, and excerpts can be created in large quantities for special needs. For more information contact the publisher:

Published by Schiffer Publishing Ltd.
4880 Lower Valley Road
Atglen, PA 19310
Phone: (610) 593-1777; Fax: (610) 593-2002
E-mail: Info@schifferbooks.com

For the largest selection of fine reference books on this and related subjects, please visit our web site at **www.schifferbooks.com**
We are always looking for people to write books on new and related subjects. If you have an idea for a book please contact us at the above address.

This book may be purchased from the publisher. Include $5.00 for shipping. Please try your bookstore first. You may write for a free catalog.

In Europe, Schiffer books are distributed by
Bushwood Books
6 Marksbury Ave.
Kew Gardens
Surrey TW9 4JF England
Phone: 44 (0) 20 8392-8585; Fax: 44 (0) 20 8392-9876
E-mail: info@bushwoodbooks.co.uk
Website: www.bushwoodbooks.co.uk

Type set in !Sketchy Times/Brisa Alternates/New Baskerville BT

ISBN: 978-0-7643-3613-3
Printed in The United States of America

Contents

Two Witches... 5

Introduction... 7

Part One: The Birth of Witchcraft....................... 10
   The Pagan World.. 11
   The Witch Craze Around the World 13

Part Two: Roots... 35
   Wiccan, Pagan, Witch, What? 36
   Our Mothers of the Craft 42
   Our Fathers of the Craft 79

Part Three: Twenty-First Century Witchcraft 109
   Being a Solitary 110
   Covens 111

Part Four: Spells, Chants, and Rituals 115
   Magick of the Elders 116
   Spells and Rituals 117
   Chants 122
   Modern-Day Spells, Rituals, and Chants 125
   Contributor Biographies 148

A Final Word 150

Resources 151

Books of the Elders 155

Books of the Modern Witch 156

Bibliography 158

Dedication

To all of my brothers and sisters of the Craft, and to Laurie Cabot who embraced my soul with her wonderful stories, life, teachings, and magick.

Acknowledgments

I would like to thank Schiffer Publishing for always having such faith in my writing and book ideas. A special thanks to Peter Schiffer and Dinah Roseberry, You're both the best! Thanks to The Museum of Witchcraft and Patricia Crowther for allowing me to use the picture of Gerald Gardner's handmade sword. Thanks to Gillian Moy for the use of Sybil Leeks old storefront picture. Thanks to Tof who allowed me the use of the Witches Mill picture, and is the author of *Gerald Gardener et le Culte des Sorcières*. Thank you to Melissa Harrington and Melissa Seims for the great newspaper articles on Sybil Leek, Gerald Gardner, and Doreen Valiente. Also thank you to Gypsy for allowing me to use the lyrics to "Two Witches"– I love that song and it means a lot. Thank you to my dear friend, Marla Brooks, for her wonderful spells for animals. Thanks to my sisters of the Craft Macha Raven Mare, Rev. Branwyn Willows HPs, and Lady Springwolf for allowing me to share such great spells, rituals, and herbals with the world! Personal thanks to Laurie Cabot for her wonderful interview; you are such an inspiration to many. Thank You!

Two Witches

There was a wise woman lived by the sea
Great was her power a Witch was she
Her hair black as night
Her eyes green as malachite
Her life filled with magick and prophecy

While in the same town in another part
A woman of song with love in her heart
Weaving musical rhymes round those, she knew in her time
Was led by Diana into the Art

The Witch taught the Chantress her Mysteries
And they practiced the wonders of witchery
In circles of light two women worked through the night
With colors and numbers and imagery.

Then one day Diana did so decide
This woman of song had to turn aside
From her friend by the sea and find answers inwardly
A magickal dream was to be her guide to the answers inside.
As the Chantress went into her dreams that night
Diana sent visions in sparkling light
'Come awake, now arise, call to Sisters with fiery eyes'
Saying that truth is not black or white

And then through the dream mist a white light shone
On the wings of a Raven perched upon a throne
'A magician am I' he said and he winked an eye
'Love casts out fear you are not alone'

He said 'there is a magickal place I know'
'Take a ride on my back and away we'll go'
Their journey was short
They soon arrived in the outer court
Of the wizard who lives where the four winds blow

The Wizard said Chantress revealeth thy name
To the Goddess and Gods be it so ordain
To the old ones to the winds as a witch your life will begin
When you drink from this cup while the candles flame

She drank from the cup and her name she told
To the Goddess and Guardians and Gods of old
A pentacle of power she received in that magick hour
Made by the Raven from silver and gold
Silver and gold

Then from the East, North, South, West and beyond
Swept four winds and the wizard and raven were gone
In a crystal, she saw herself asleep as she was before
Asleep in the moonlight but not alone

For someone was standing beside her bed 'twas the goddess Diana
Softly she said 'I am Queen of the Wise
I'm within I see through your eyes
As I am the weaver, you are the thread

When a dream dreams the dreamer the dreams the reel
When a song sings the singer, a spell is revealed
As she saw herself, there the dream began to disappear
And the Chantress returned from beyond the veil

~Lyrics by: Gypsy, *Enchantress* (1990)

Introduction

What is our fascination with the word Witch? We can look back throughout history during the burning times for example, and see just how our ancestors and society greatly misunderstood just what the word or being a "witch" really meant. Could it be that these magical individuals hold some form of understanding and knowledge about the great cosmic mysteries? Do witches possess the powers to heal and see into our futures? Perhaps...but I can tell you from firsthand experience that whatever mystical abilities these fascinating practitioners hold, they are just like you and I. Some are doctors, lawyers, mechanics, teachers, accountants, grocery clerks, and they deserve respect.

Why is our society so scared of witches, yet during the Halloween season, people flock like sheep to every witch shop or event that highlights witches. I have personally witnessed a line of individuals of all ages wait three hours to enter a Witch shop during Halloween season in the town of Salem, Massachusetts—three hours to hopefully get a glimpse of Laurie Cabot, who is Salem's famous witch. Such people, like my mother (many, many, years ago), who was a staunch Roman Catholic but still determined "to see what all the fuss was about" and sneak a peek at a real witch during the height of the Halloween season. If one visits the city of Salem today, over 400 witches live and work in or around that fine metropolitan area. And this is just one city.

Over the years, I have come to meet some wonderful individuals who are witches and some are my friends. These individuals invited me into their lives and homes with such openness and warmth, it was a feeling that cannot be explained in any other way except: *"It felt like coming home."* Coming home...to my own long forgotten roots.

Even still, in today's more open-minded society, those who are living the life and practicing witchcraft are still the victims of those uneducated individuals who will not try to get past their own fears. Yet, the same individuals who shout out nasty names and comments will visit a witch if they need healing or insight on a personal matter. Many witches today still keep their identity secret due to being afraid of losing their jobs at a workplace or having their children seriously hurt or taken away. Why is it wrong for witches to wear their pentacles or a symbols of their faith out in public? But for a practitioner of a mainstream faith, such as

Christianity, Judaism, Buddhism, etc., they wear their declaration of faith freely without fear of persecution or harassment. During my years as a Corrections Officer for a State Prison, I quickly came to realize that the inmates have full religious rights, which also covered being a Wiccan or Witch. These inmates are by law allowed to wear their religious artifacts and relics outside their shirts. Society seems to forget that witches are hard-working tax-paying citizens, too.

Over the centuries, witches have been given a bad rap and have become stereotyped as "evil" beings. I think it is time to set that record straight, don't you? Witches are people too and they have feelings.

I do need to make some major points about "witches" very clear before moving onto the next pages of this book. Witches are NOT evil nor do they personally believe in evil, hell, or Satan and demons (as a matter of fact, when I showed Laurie Cabot my book *Devils and Demonology* she laughed, but wanted a signed copy, which meant a lot.) Witches take time out of their lives (just like everyone else) to clean up OUR environment, being activists for children and animals, feeding the hungry, giving clothes to the needy, and giving shelter to the homeless. How are witches so evil then?

I've always had a focus on education and this book is no different; you will soon come to realize that I speak my mind and

Detail of religion mural in lunette from the Family and Education series by Charles Sprague Pearce. North Corridor, Great Hall, Library of Congress Thomas Jefferson Building, Washington, D.C. Artist is Charles Sprague Pearce 1896.

say it like it is. This book has brought me through the gamut emotionally, from researching the burning times to reading about steps toward freedom for the religion. I am hoping to shed light on a few individuals who I truly feel helped through activism and awareness to spread the word of witchcraft and help rectify all of the negative propaganda that has been pushed upon the masses for centuries regarding the Old Religion.

Not all of our history is lost, especially our recent history; religious freedom fighters continue to send out pamphlets and protest. The witchcraft movement has not ended; I realized during the process of writing this book that this is no time to sit back and enjoy the fruits of our foremothers' and forefathers' labor. It is a time to continue their work, make a stand for the religion, and help to bring witchcraft into the pantheon of respectable world religions.

1

The Birth

of

Witchcraft

The Pagan World

In his cool hall, with haggard eyes,
The Roman noble lay;
He drove abroad, in furious guise,
Along the Appian way.

He made a feast, drank fierce and fast,
And crowned his hair with flowers—
No easier nor no quicker passed
The impracticable hours.

The brooding East with awe beheld
Her impious younger world.
The Roman tempest swelled and swelled,
And on her head was hurled.

The East bowed low before the blast
In patient, deep disdain;
She let the legions thunder past,
And plunged in thought again.

So well she mused, a morning broke
Across her spirit grey;
A conquering, new-born joy awoke,
And filled her life with day.

"Poor world," she cried, "so deep accurst
That runn'st from pole to pole
To seek a draught to slake thy thirst—
Go, seek it in thy soul!"

She heard it, the victorious West,
In crown and sword arrayed!
She felt the void which mined her breast,
She shivered and obeyed.

She veiled her eagles, snapped her sword,
And laid her sceptre down;
Her stately purple she abhorred,
And her imperial crown.

She broke her flutes, she stopped her sports,
Her artists could not please;
She tore her books, she shut her courts,
She fled her palaces;

Lust of the eye and pride of life
She left it all behind,
And hurried, torn with inward strife,
The wilderness to find.

Tears washed the trouble from her face!
She changed into a child!
Mid weeds and wrecks she stood—a place
Of ruin—but she smiled!

~Poet Matthew Arnold

The Witch Craze
Around the World

The only religion that England has ever given the world:
modern pagan witchcraft.

~Dr. Ron Hutton
Triumph of the Moon

When people hear me talk about the witch trials or the burning times they usually think I'm talking about the past. It is still happening people! It is not something that just happened a hundred, two hundred, or three hundred years ago. Everyday people are being sacrificed for their religious freedoms or are being "pinned" with the word *witch* as if it is a bad thing and paying the price with their lives. Yes, back in the day there were masses of people being hung, burned, tortured, and killed because of this "terrible and vile" word *witch*. But for us to believe that things are different now, to live in a state of oblivious love and worship of Deity is to ignore the call of the hundreds and thousands that still suffer.

I believe we have to look at our past so we may learn and move forward into the future with confidence. This includes looking at our mistakes and the mistakes of others. First, let's look back.

A Time Line

Before and During the 10th Century

During this time, there was great belief among the "uncultured" peasants that witches did indeed exist. The populous believed that witches were usually women, and that they practiced evil magick, putting curses on people, towns, and even someone's livestock. It was during this time that the Church began to use propaganda to denounce witches and spells as non-existent folklore and a superstitious belief system.

For example, the 5th century Synod of St. Patrick ruled that "A Christian who believes that there is a vampire in the world, that is to say, a witch, is to be anathematized; whoever lays that reputation

Weekend magazine June 24-26, 1957. *Courtesy of Melissa Harrington and Melissa Seims.*

upon a living being shall not be received into the Church until he revokes with his own voice the crime that he has committed." *A capitulary from Saxony (775-790 CE) blamed these stereotypes on pagan belief systems:* If anyone, deceived by the Devil, believes after the manner of the Pagans that any man or woman is a witch and eats men, and if on this account he burns [the alleged witch]... he shall be punished by capital sentence.

In 906 CE, the Church created the *Canon Episcopi*, a document that further outlined the inane belief in witches and witchcraft, although it did admit that some less mentally stable women believed that they flew at night with the Goddess Diana. In 975, we can still see the effects of the *Canon Episcopi*. Confessions of Egbert outlined some of the rather relaxed (compared to the later periods) laws surrounding witchcraft. (See 15th and 16th Century)

> If a woman works witchcraft and enchantment and [uses] magical philters, she shall fast for twelve months...If she kills anyone by her philters, she shall fast for seven years.

13th and 14th Century

A group of Gnostic Christians called the Cathar began gaining popularity in France. The Church, fearful, immediately declared them heretics in the year 1203. Pope Innocent III approved the trial and inquisition of the Cathar. Pope Innocent III then went on in 1252 to authorize the use of torture during the inquisition trials. This of course, greatly increased the conviction rate. In 1258, Pope Alexander IV created a mandate that inquisitors only take cases of true heresy. They were not to touch ones of sorcery or divination, unless heresy was a part of it. In 1326, the Church began to allow the investigators to look further into witchcraft as a charge of heresy; this included divination, and sorcery. They also began to develop the theory regarding witches and Satan. By 1340, the beliefs regarding witches had come to include the idea that they were in league with Satan, were whores of the Devil, and also that they would kidnap and eat children or offer them as sacrifice to their evil God. During the time of the Black Plague (late 1340s), witches were actually accused of poisoning the wells and causing the scourge.

15th and 16th Century

Christian theologians begin to write papers which proved the existence of witchcraft in the early 1400s. The *Formicarus* was written by Nider relaying the persecution of a man for witchcraft; this would eventually be added to the *Malleus Maleficarum*. In the year 1450, the witch-hunts began in force; the Church capitalized on the myths surrounding witchcraft since pre-Christian times, emphasizing the negative point of view. They furthered the myth that witches ate babies, sold their souls to demons, and threatened men with impotence or infertility. Recent religious theologians and historians have come to believe that the Church wanted to have the monopoly on religion. In that same year, Gutenberg created the printing press, allowing the anti-witch propaganda to spread at even higher levels. Pope Innocent VIII issued a new Papal Bull in 1484 condoning the act of hunting down and killing Satan's cohorts.

In the late 1480s the *Malleus Maleficarum* was created—the name literally translates into *The Witches Hammer*. It talks about the art of extracting confessions from the reluctant guilty. In 1517, Martin Luther, a leader in the Reformation, nailed ninety-five theses (these papers were actually called "Disputation on the Power and Efficacy of Indulgences" to a cathedral door in Wittenberg, Germany, on Halloween night. These papers showed the corruption within the Church; with power came greed and even Martin Luther could not escape it. His repentance came in the form of these letters; he also suffered mortification of the body in order to be forgiven for his sins. There were literally ninety-five disputations upon the document itself. Here you can read some of the excerpts from Martin Luther's theses translated from the original Latin:

MALLEVS MALEFICARVM,

MALEFICAS ET EARVM

· hæresim frameâ conterens ,

EX VARIIS AVCTORIBVS COMPILATVS,
& in quatuor Tomos iustè distributus ,

QVORVM DVO PRIORES VANAS DÆMONVM
versutias , præstigiosas eorum delusiones , superstitiosas Strigimagarum
cæremonias , horrendos etiam cum illis congressus ; exactam denique
tam pestiferæ sectæ disquisitionem , & punitionem complectuntur.
Tertius praxim Exorcistarum ad Dæmonum , & Strigimagarum male-
ficia de Christi fidelibus pellenda ; Quartus verò Artem Doctrinalem,
Benedictionalem , & Exorcismalem continent.

TOMVS PRIMVS.

Indices Auctorum , capitum , rerúmque non desunt,

Editio nouissima , infinitis penè mendis expurgata ; cuíque accessit Fuga
Dæmonum & Complementum artis exorcisticæ.

Vir sine mulier, in quibus Pythonicus, vel divinationis fuerit spiritus, morte moriatur ;
Leuitici cap. 10.

LVGDVNI ,
Sumptibus CLAVDII BOVRGEAT, sub signo Mercurij Galli.

M. DC. LXIX.
CVM PRIVILEGIO REGIS.

Title page of the seventh Cologne edition of the *Malleus Maleficarum,* 1520 (from the University of Sydney Library).

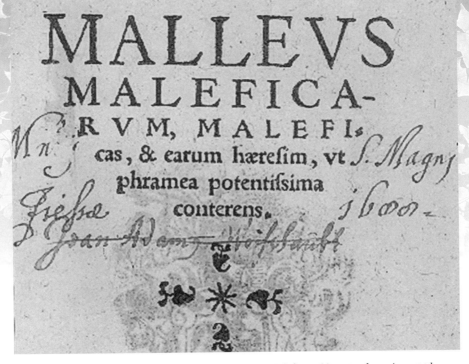

MALLEVS
MALEFICA-
RVM, MALEFI,
cas, & earum hæresim, vt S. Magni
phramea potentissima
conterens.

The Latin title is "*MALLEUS MALEFICARUM, Maleficas, & earum hæresim, ut ph-ramea potentissima conterens.*" (English: The Hammer of Witches, which destroyeth Witches and their heresy like a most powerful spear.)

35. They preach no Christian doctrine who teach that contrition is not necessary in those who intend to buy souls out of purgatory or to buy confessionalia.

72. But he who guards against the lust and license of the pardon-preachers, let him be blessed! (In this he is referring to those priests and preachers within the Church who "for a price" could get you out of having to live in purgatory).

92. Away, then, with all those prophets who say to the people of Christ, "Peace, peace," and there is no peace!

Some speculate that it never happened, but it can be proven that he did write a letter to his superiors that day, forsaking the payment for indulgences and that he'd attached the ninety-five theses to the letter. Either way, it helped to push the reformation, allowing for different branches of the religion to be created, and become Christianity as we see it today.

In countries that mainly practiced Roman Catholicism, the burnings continued in earnest, and with the Protestants, the witches were mainly hung. In England, they did not torture nearly as much as in places such as Germany, so their death rate was seemingly low at only nineteen percent. In contrast, Germany made up for almost half of the deaths by the end of the burning times, adding up the body count to around 25,000 tried, convicted, and killed. In 1563, renowned occult writer Johann Weyer wrote the book *De Praestigiis Daemonum;* in it he renounced the belief in witches. He believed that the witch craze was a method used by Satan to turn man against his brothers and sisters. He also wrote that he believed confession by torture to be absolutely useless and would reject any confessions that came from such practices. The church actually did not have a lot to do with trials themselves; the bulk of them were held in secular courts. In the other extreme, in 1580, a book entitled *De la Demonomanie des Sorciers* was written; inside, the author Jean Bodin speaks on how he believes that all witches should be punished—both to appease God and avoid his wrath and for the safety of the people. He thought that if there was even the flimsiest piece of evidence, better to kill or punish and be sure than to let the witch trick you and pay the price later.

17th and 18th Century

The trials reached a peak between 1550 and 1650. These next hundred years saw the execution of so many people; and cats during this time too nearly became extinct because of their connection to witchcraft as familiars. In 1608, Francesco Guazzo wrote the *Compendium Maleficarum;* it spoke on the pacts made with Satan and the magick witches used to harm other people. A panic hit the Basque area of Spain during the early 1600s, but the inquisition put out an *Edict of Silence* banning all discussions of witchcraft. This calmed the crowds in Basque and the threat soon died down. A second craze began in Vizcaya. Again the Inquisition put into action an *Edict of Silence,* but this time the King refused to acknowledge the edict and burned alive somewhere around 300 people. In 1631, a Jesuit priest wrote another book condemning the witch trials in Wurzburg, Germany. He proclaimed them an abomination and that the victims only confessed because of the sadistic tortures that they were subjected to.

In 1642, the first witch hanging occurred. I'm going to set this timeline on its ear a little bit because I really want to discuss this part. Most people think that Salem was the first hanging; it was not. It was the most *popularized* hanging. I know that many of my readers will most likely be in the USA, so I think it is important for American witches to know their roots and history. So here it goes.

THE DEVON WITCHES
IN MEMORY OF
Temperance Lloyd
Susannah Edwards
Mary Trembles
OF BIDEFORD DIED 1682
Alice Molland
DIED 1685
THE LAST PEOPLE IN ENGLAND
TO BE EXECUTED FOR WITCHCRAFT
TRIED HERE & HANGED AT HEAVITREE
In the hope of an end to persecution & intolerance

A plaque commemorating the last executions for witchcraft in England.

The first witch trial in the United States occurred in Connecticut. Now let us please remember that at this time we were still a colony under British rule; we had not separated yet and were still subjects of the Kings Law. Writer R.G. Tomlinson talks about the hysteria and the first hanging in his book *Witchcraft Trials of Connecticut.*

In 1642 witchcraft was punishable by death in Connecticut. This capital offense was backed by references to the Bible, i.e., Ex: 22, 18; Lev: 20, 27; Deu: 18, 10, 11. ***Alse Young (sometimes also referred to as Achsah or Alice) of Windsor, Connecticut was the first person executed for witchcraft in America.*** Alse was hanged at Meeting House Square in Hartford on what is now the site of the Old State House. A journal of then Massachusetts Governor John Winthrop states that "One of Windsor was hanged." The second town clerk of Windsor, Matthew Grant also confirms the execution with the May 26, 1647 diary entry, "Alse Young was hanged."

Although Connecticut may not have experienced the same level of hysteria as Salem Massachusetts, Alse Young was not the last person hanged for witchcraft. Mary Johnson of Wethersfield was executed in 1648 after having confessed to entering into a compact with the devil. Joan and John Carrington also of Wethersfield were executed in 1651. Rebecca and Nathaniel Greensmith and Mary Barnes were found guilty of witchcraft and were hanged in Hartford on January 25, 1663. Ann Cole had accused Rebecca Greensmith of making her have strange fits. Witchcraft was last listed as a capital crime in 1715. The crime of witchcraft disappeared from the list of capital crimes when the laws were next printed in 1750.

The charges leveled against Also Young were taken from the Bible so I decided to look at exactly what she was being executed for. I used the *American Standard Bible*, so I would not be surprised if the wording was different, but the essence of the message communicated is much the same.

In Leviticus 20:27 it states:

A man also or a woman that hath a familiar spirit, or that is a wizard, shall surely be put to death: they shall stone them with stones; their blood shall be upon them.

And then in Deuteronomy 18:10-11:

There shall not be found with thee any one that maketh his son or his daughter to pass through the fire, one that useth divination, one that practiseth augury, or an enchanter, or a sorcerer, or charmer, or a consulter with a familiar spirit, or a wizard, or a necromancer.

I saved this one for last because I wanted to talk about it a little bit. In Exodus 20:18 it states:

*Thou shalt not suffer **a witch** to live.*

Well, that's pretty plain spoke. Let's look at this for a moment. Now take the original text for witch or sorceress. In 1584, Sir Walter Scott wrote the book *Discoverie of Witchcraft;* in it, he basically debunks the tenet and shows the true meaning behind it. I was lucky enough to stumble upon a second edition circa 1886 of the book, which had so fumed King James I that he had the book burned all across his country. This is taken from the chapter titled, "The Sixt Booke, the first chapter:"

The exposition of this Hebrue word Chasaph, wherein is answered the objection conteined in Exodus 22. to wit: Thou shalt not suffer a witch to live, and of Simon Magus. Acts. 8.

CHASAPH, being an Hebrue word, is Latined Veneficiuni, and is in English, poisoning, or witchcraft; if you will so have it. The Hebrue sentence written in Exodus., 22. is by the 70. interpretors translated thus into Greeke, Φάρμακδυς όυκ ἘΠιξεώσετε, which in Latine is, Veneficos (sive) venieficas non retifiebitis in vita, in English, You shall not suffer anie poisoners, or (as it is translated) witches to live. The which sentence Josephus, an Hebrue borne, and a man of great estimation, learning and fame, interpreteth in this wise; Let none of the children of Israel have any poison that is deadlie, or prepared to anie hurtfull use. If anie be apprehended with such stuffe, let him be put to death, and suffer that which he ment to doo to them, for whom he prepared it. The Rabbins exposition agree heerewithall. Lex Cornelia differeth not from this sense, to wit, that he must suffer death, which either maketh, selleth, or hath anie poison, to the intent to kill anie man. This word is found in these places following: Exodus. 22, 18. Deut. 18, 10. 2. Sam. 9, 22. Dan. 2, 2. 2. Chr. 2, 6. Esay. 47, 9, 12. Malach, 3, 5. Jerem.27, 9. Mich. 5, 2. Nah. 3, 4. bis. Howbeit, in all our English / translations, Chasaph is translated, witchcraft.

But why would King James I want to change the meaning of poisoner to witch? What made him so phobic about the possibilities of witches? Supposedly, it was his brush with the Berwick witches. Prior to becoming King James I of England, he was King James the VI of Scotland. In the year 1590, King James was on his way home and bringing his new Queen, Anne of Denmark, with him; they traveled by sea, crossing the Atlantic. At that same time, around 200 witches gathered in a decrepit and abandoned church called St. Andrews in North Berwick. Their goal? To kill the king. They wanted to conjure a storm that would sink the King's ship, sending him into the abyss forevermore and his new Queen with him.

Here is how it all went down, in legend anyway. The witches burnt a cat and then mutilated a corpse removing the hands, feet, and genitalia. They were then attached to the charred corpse of the cat which they then threw into the sea. After this was done, the sky turned black and the "devil" unleashed his reign upon the sea. Storms and huge waves crashed in the ocean. However, King James' ship sailed safely through it. The witches plot was foiled.

An investigation started in Edinburgh into the possibility that witchcraft was initiated after some tips about the "coven's" meeting. Now I use the term coven loosely in this situation, as I do not want witches misrepresented. From a historic point, it's very interesting but the acceptance of witchcraft in modern society is still tenuous at best. There are no covens that I know of that use bad magick—if they did, then they certainly could not call themselves witches.

But I digress, so the investigation carried on until a witch named Gilly Duncan confessed to being in cahoots with the devil; she then named a few other witches. One thing led to another and eventually seventy people were accused and tried on the crime of using witchcraft in an attempt to kill the King. One of the seventy was no one less than the fifth Earl of Bothwell, Agnes. Another of the accused claimed that the devil had taught them how to conjure the storm.

This was the first major witch trial in Scotland.

Back to the history, shall we? Our next major event is one that every good witch knows about. It is the hangings in Salem, Massachusetts. Again, the United States had not yet formed and we were colonists for the empire. I would like to present a couple of different articles to you. One is the deposition of James Kettle against Sarah Bishop; it goes as follows.

The deposition of James Kettle aged twentyseven years or there about testyfieth & saith that I was att Docter

Salem Witch Trials Memorial.

Grigs his hous on the tenth of this instant may & there saw Elizebeth Hubbard in severall Fitts: and after her fits ware over she told me that she saw my two Childdren Laying before her & that thay cry'd for vengance & that Sarah Bishop bid her Look on them & said that she kiled them & and thay were by her description much as they were when they ware put in to there Coffins (to) be buried & she told me that Sarah bishop told her that I was going to burn akiln of potts & that she would break them if she Could: & i took notice that while she was in her Fitts that she Cried & held her apron before her face saying that she would not se them Docter Grigs & his wife and John hues ware thare present.

Next I am going to show you the case of Mary Bradbury, first her Indictment given July 2nd 1692.

Gallows Hill, Salem, Massachusetts.

Ss The Juriors for our Sover' Lord & Lady the King and Queen doe present That Mary Bradbury Wife of Capt Thomas Bradbury of Salisbury In the County of Essex Gent m upon the Second day of July In the yeare aforesaid and divers other days and times as well before as after certaine detestable arts called Witchcraft and Sorceries Wickedly Mallitiously and felloniously hath used practised and Exercised at and in the Towne of Salem in the County aforesaid in up on & against one Sarah Vibber Wife of John Vibber of Salem afore-said Husbandman by which said wicked acts the said Sarah Vibber the second day of July aforesaid & divers other days and times both before and after was and is Tortured Afflicted Consumed Pined Wasted & Tormented & also for sundry other acts of Witchcraft by the said Mary Bradbury Comitted Acted and done before and since *that time against the peace of our Sov'r Lord & Lady the King and Queene theire Crowne and Dignity and the forme Of the Stattute In that case made and Provided Witness*

Mary Walcott

Eliz. Hobard

Eliz. Booth

Mercy lewis

(Reverse) Indictmt. Bradbury – *Vibber bil a vera*

Her answer to this indictment was firm and unswerving. I believe her words wholeheartedly, and honestly, I feel you cannot prove whether anyone burned or tortured during the witch trials were witches or not. During those times, the witches hid so well; they hid in abbeys, in the fields working next to good Christians. They had learned the need to hide their faith over the years and it became second nature, which is why to this day I still believe that many within the craft still hide, they wear their pentacles under their shirts and don't bring attention to themselves. Many think that the witches we see in newspapers and on television are the majority, but they are the minority.

Back to our victim's answer to her indictment:

The Answer of Mary Bradbury in the charge of Witchcraft or familliarity with the Divell I doe plead not guilty.

I am wholly inocent of any such wickedness through the goodness of god that have kept mee hitherto) I am the servant of Jesus Christ & Have given my self up to him as my only lord & saviour: and to the dilligent attendance upon him in all his holy ordinances, in utter contempt & defiance of the divell, and all his works as horid & detestible; and accordingly have endevo'red to frame my life; & conversation according to the

An old drawing of the death of Giles Corey (September 19, 1692) by being pressed with heavy stones after conviction as a witch during the Salem Witch Trials. (Artist of drawing is unknown.)

rules of his holy word, & in that faith & practise resolve by the help and assistance of god to contineu to my lifes end: for the truth of what I say as to matter of practiss I humbly refer my self, to my brethren & neighbors that know mee and unto the searcher of all hearts for the truth & uprightness of my heart therein: (human frailties, & unavoydable infirmities excepted) of which i bitterly complayne every day.

Mary Bradbury

Mary's husband spoke up for her; so did the local pastor, James Allin, William Carr, Robert and John Pike. The number of people who testified for her character came to be about one hundred. Each spoke of her love of the ministry, family (of which there were eleven children and four grandchildren), and community. Nevertheless, the opposition was overwhelming. Samuel Endicott gave his own story.

Burning of three witches in Baden, Switzerland (1585) by Johann Jakob Wick.

Sam'll Endecott aged thirty one years or thereabout Testifies That about eleven years since being bound upon a vioage to sea w'th Capt Sam'll Smith Late of Boston Diceas'd, just before we sayl'd mrs Bradbery of Salisbury the prisoner now att the barr came to Boston w'th some firkins of butter of w'ch Capt Smith bought two, one of them proved halfe way butter and after wee had been att sea three weekes our men. were nott able to eat itt, itt stanck soe and runn w'th magotts, w'ch made the men very much disturb'd about itt and would often say thatt they heard mrs Bradbury was a witch and thatt they verily beleived she was soe or else she would nott

have served the Capt soe as to sell him such butter. And further this
deponent Testifieth that in four dayes after they sett sayle they mett
w'th such a violent storm that we lost our main mast and riggin & Lost
fifeteen horses and thatt about a fortnight after we sett our jury mast
and thatt very night there came up a Shipp by our side and Carried
away two of the mizon shrouds and one of the Leaches of the mainsaile:
and this deponent further sayth thatt after they arived att Barbados
and went to Saltitudos & had Laden their vessell the next morning she
sprang a leake in the hold w'ch wasted seurall tunns of salt in soe much
thatt we were forct to unlade our vessell again wholy to stopp our leake
there was then four foot of water in the hold after we had taken in
our lading again we had a good passage home butt when we came near
the Land the Capt sent this deponent forward to looke out for land in
a bright moone shining night and as he was sitting upon the windless
he heard a Rumbling noise under him w'th thatt he the s'd deponent
Testifieth Thatt he looked one the side of the windless and saw the
leggs of some pson being no wayes frighted & Thatt presently he was
shook and looked over his shoulder, & saw the appearance of a woman
from her middle upwards, haveing a white Capp and white neckcloth
on her, w'ch then affrighted him very much, and as he was turning
of the indless he saw the aforsaid two leggs.

Jurat in Curia Sep'r 9'th 1692
(Reverse) Sam. Endecott

After Samuel, nine other people spoke out against her, including
family of William Carr. Mary was convicted of witchcraft and sentenced
to execution by hanging. But the story does not end there. Thanks to
ongoing pushes from her friends, Mary's execution was delayed repeat-

edly. After the witch craze had passed, she was released, and died in her bed December 20th, 1700. The heirs of Mary Bradbury received £20 in 1711 for the pain and suffering Mary had gone through during the witch trials. Also in 1711, the courts expunged the names of twenty-two of the thirty-one accused witches. Later in 1957, the Commonwealth cleared the others. Many believe that the witch trials were due to a chemical in the rye that was grown that year; others feel it was mass hysteria. I do not know which, but I have had the opportunity to stand where they were hung, to walk where they are buried, and I can tell you, I don't feel they've left yet. I do not know that they ever will.

In 1745, 1775, and 1782 France, Germany, and Switzerland (in that order) stopped the witch trials. In 1792, Poland executed its last witch, and in 1830, the Church ceased the execution of witches in South America. Finally, everyone breathed a sigh of relief thinking that the curse of the witch craze was over. If only. There would still be isolated incidents of witch lynches in Europe and America until the 20th century. However, even after that, the degradation and stigma of the word *witch* continued to haunt many of its practitioners. They no longer would utter the word but would hide beneath a faith that was not their own.

Witch Craze in the 20th Century

Europe and Eastern Continents: So now we are brought up to the 20th century, a time of industrialism and technology, hard science clashing with spiritualism. You probably think I'm talking about the Victorian era; well I'm not. The Witch craze that swept through the Middle Ages in Europe continues to this day throughout the world. As late as 2010, I read an article in *Mysteries* Magazine that questioned:

> "What would have happened if the Salem Witch Trials had been televised? Would there have been outrage from those who saw it happening and could they have stopped the panic before it spun out of control?
>
> "Video was recently shot of five women in the Deoghar district of the state of Jharkand, India, who were accused of witchcraft by a local cleric. The footage, which shows them being dragged from their huts, paraded naked, beaten, and forced to eat human excrement, has caused outrage throughout the subcontinent.
>
> "Four people have been arrested for their involvement and the victims are receiving police protection.
>
> "It is believed that hundreds of people, mostly women, have been killed in India because they were thought to be witches. Experts say that superstition is largely responsible, but in some cases 'witches,' particularly widows, are targeted for their land and property."

India is a more rural area, with so many sublets and many of the villages would be considered "backward" compared to our own technological advances. Life is simple and still hearkens back to time before technology, where candles and torches still lit the way and where religion, agriculture, and family were the prominent focuses in everyone's life. But what about in Scotland?

In 1944, Helen Duncan was arrested for witchcraft—that is 209 years *after* the passing of the Witchcraft Act in 1735. Why was she arrested? Helen Duncan was a medium. She liked to hold séances; she did quite frequently in fact. As the wife of a cabinetmaker they moved around a bit, eventually landing in Portsmouth where they made their home. It also happened to be where the base for the Royal Navy was during the Second World War. The year was 1941 and Helen was holding a séance; this one would prove to be a turning point for her. During the session, a male spirit came through; he was a sailor and his message was simple. He had just died on a ship called *Barnham*.

The sinking of this military ship was not to be announced for another few months, as the government knew it would lower moral. Helen carried on with life, and then on January 19th, 1944, three years after this incident, Helen was holding yet another séance when some plain-clothed police officers and a naval lieutenant came in and arrested Helen and three of her audience members. The government was afraid that she would eventually spill the beans about D-Day, which was in its final stages of discussion and execution. She was initially charged with conspiracy and being a spy, but later that charge was changed to contravening the Witchcraft Act of 1735 by "pretending to raise the spirits of the dead."

Forty-four witnesses, including a justice of the peace and a few journalists, spoke in her defense; still she was found guilty. Even her right to appeal the judgment was taken away from her. She spent nine months in Holloway.

Finally, Churchill, already interested in spiritualism, fought to repeal the Witchcraft Act. Helen was eventually released from prison, but was continually harassed by the law enforcement. In 1956, again the police, looking for evidence of fraud, of which they found none, bombarded her séance. Their treatment of her was so rough whilst in a trance state, that many believe it led directly to her death in December of that same year, less than five weeks after the incident.

An article run in the *UK Guardian* January 13th, 2007, talks about Mary Martin and her fight to clear her grandmother's name:

> Mary Martin was 11 years old when her father taught her to box. She would come home from school scratched and bruised, her

ears ringing with abuse from the playground. Mary Martin had the unhappy distinction of being the granddaughter of Britain's last convicted witch.

Mrs. Martin knew her grandmother, Helen Duncan, as a comforting woman she could trust, the granny with a special gift: talking to spirits. But this was April 1944, at the height of the war with Germany. Mrs. Duncan had just been branded by an Old Bailey jury as a witch and spy guilty of revealing wartime secrets.

Some 50 years after Mrs. Duncan's death, a fresh campaign has been launched to clear her name, with a petition calling on the home secretary, John Reid, to grant a posthumous pardon. Her conviction, said Mrs. Martin, was simply "ludicrous."

The appeal is winning international support from experts in perhaps the world's most infamous witch trial: the conviction and execution of 20 girls, men and women at Salem, Massachusetts, in 1692. "Helen Duncan was very much victimised by her times, and she too suffered," said Alison D'Amario, education director at the Salem Witch Museum.

The fight still goes on today, with thousands of people signing the on-line petitions to free Helen Duncan's name.

Here is a list of more recent offenses from the UK, and Greece:

In 2003, a teacher at Shawlands Academy in Glasgow was not allowed to take time off with pay to attend a Druid rite, while members of others religions were allowed the privilege.

In 2007, a Brighton teacher's assistant was allegedly fired for being wiccan.

According to Greek Law No 1363/38, with amendment Law No. 1672/39, "Anyone engaging in proselytism shall be liable to imprisonment and a fine between 1,000 and 50,000 drachmas; he shall, moreover be subject to police supervision for a period of between six months and one year to be fixed by the court when convicting the offender." The second law requires anybody who is not an Orthodox Christian to obtain a "church license" from both the Ministry of Education and Religious Affairs and the local Orthodox bishops, but only the Orthodox Church, Judaism and Islam are recognized as "legal persons of public law." According to a press release from *The Supreme Council of Gentile Hellenes,* there have been threats against the life of its members and a bookstore burning.

Witch Craze in 20th Century America: Bigotry and closed minds are hard things to fight. But you can. What witches need is not oppression, but publicists! There was in article back in 1999 from the *Star-Telegram* based around soldiers who practiced Wicca or witchcraft:

> FORT HOOD — In flowing capes...plain black T-shirts, civilians and off-duty soldiers joined ands and jumped a smoldering bonfire after worshipping pagan deities, sipping homemade honey wine and consuming ears of corn.
>
> "We are a circle within a circle with no beginning and never ending," intoned 60 men, women, and children encircling the blaze. "Horned one, lover son, leaper in the corn, deep in the mother, die and be reborn," they chanted to the god Pan.
>
> These are the witches...of Fort Hood, the nation's largest military base....home to 42,000 troops.
>
> Headquarters of III Corps, which includes the 4th Infantry Division (Mechanized), known as "Hell on Wheels," and the 1st Cavalry Division.
>
> The Wiccans' full-moon rites at the on-base campsite, used on other days by Boy Scouts and Girl Scouts, have generated international headlines – "Onward Pagan Soldiers," read one in Britain – as well as heat from religious conservatives, Sen. Strom Thurmond, R-S.C., and Gov. George W. Bush.
>
> "This is war," thundered the Rev. Jack Harvey of nearby Killeen, who has vowed to run the witches off base. Harvey, who has announced a Labor Day "march against wickedness," sees no difference between Wicca and devil worship. He has instructed that at least one member of his congregation carry a handgun at services – "in case a warlock tries to grab one of our kids."
>
> "I've heard they drink blood, eat babies. They have fires, they probably cook them. This is unbelievably wrong," said Harvey.

But that isn't the earliest account of bigotry against the Craft and its practitioners. The last person to be arrested (not executed) was Zsuzsanna Budapest. Her mother was a practicing witch and sculptress who supported her family through her art, much of which reflected the goddess and divine feminine. This greatly influenced her daughter who later became the founder of Dianic Wicca. Zsuzsanna would later move to the United States after the poverty hit post-war Europe. She would go on to write quite a few important tomes on witchcraft and contribute much to the feminist movement. She founded the first feminist witches coven, Susan B. Anthony Coven I. But we are not here to talk about her contributions to the women's rights movement, but to talk about her arrest for witchcraft which happened in the 1970s.

The year was 1974, and Zsuzsanna had opened a candle and bookshop called *Feminist Wicca* in Venice, California. Part of what she offered was Tarot card readings. One day in 1974, a woman came in to have her cards read. Thinking nothing of it, Budapest gave her the reading; little did she know what she was in for. Zsuzsanna was arrested for reading for her client who turned out to be an undercover police officer. Making her the last person, tried, convicted, and sentenced as a witch. Over the next nine years she made appeals to the court on the grounds that all forms of divination were a women's right to counsel each other within the context of their religion. With a pro-bono legal team, Z eventually was acquitted and the law against "fortune telling" was struck from the books in California. In 2003, Budapest was honored for her contributions by the California Institute of Integral Studies and named a Foremother of the women's spirituality movement.

Here is a list of some more recent offenses:

In 1999, in response to a statement by Representative Bob Barr (R-GA, now Libertarian) regarding Wiccan gatherings on military bases, the Free Congress Foundation called for U.S. citizens to not enlist or re-enlist in the U.S. Army until the Army terminated the on-base freedoms of religion, speech, and assembly for all Wiccan soldiers. Though this movement died a "quiet death," on 24 June 1999, then-Governor George W. Bush stated on a television news program that "I don't think witchcraft is a religion and I wish the military would take another look at this and decide against it."

In 2006, Army Chaplain Captain Donald Larsen was removed from his post in Iraq when he changed his religious affiliation from Pentacostal to Wicca and applied to be the first Wiccan military chaplain.

In 2007, a settlement between the U.S. Dept. of Veteran's Affairs and Wiccans finally made the pentacle a symbol to be engraved on the tombstones of witches. *"This settlement has forced the Bush Administration into acknowledging that there are no second class religions in America, including among our nation's veterans,"* said the Rev. Barry W. Lynn, director of Americans United for Separation of Church and State, which represented the Wiccans in the lawsuit.

We have had some wins, and many losses, but one thing I love about witches is that they are part of one religion that has survived and will continue to survive and thrive in the coming years.

2

Roots

Wiccan, Pagan, Witch, What?

Throughout my travels, talking about occultism in all of its forms (including witchcraft), I keep hearing the words *pagan* and *wiccan* being used interchangeably with the word *witch*. I remember when I started studying this religious system, my own confusion over these terminologies. You can be a pagan and be a witch and a wiccan but wiccans and pagans are not necessarily witches. Confused yet?

It reminded me of what my friend, Psychic Medium Beckah Boyd, once told me about psychics: All psychics can be mediums but not all mediums are psychic. Again, confusion ensued. But with all of these different terms about witches and pagans and wiccans being thrown around, I decided that some clarification could help us all out. So I talked to friends, scoured the internet, and leaders of various covens and groups. Each had their own ideas about what makes a wiccan a wiccan, a witch a witch, and a pagan a pagan. But the fundamentals were there for each. So let's begin.

Pagans

Everyone has their own meaning of the word pagan and each believe that their's is the correct version. This is not a unique phenomenon as even with the word "Christian," everyone has their own concept as to what it truly means. I assume this is something that happens in many different religions.

The origin of the word *pagan* comes from the Latin "paganus." There are three distinct meanings for this word. Unfortunately, there are no absolutes on the meaning of the word prior to the 5th century. None of the three meanings have garnered complete acceptance.

In our day and age, many practitioners of pagan religions believe that the word meant country dweller and was used as a derogatory term by the Christians to those who lived in more rustic communities and kept their old belief systems.

In the Roman Empire, it is believed that the term *"paganus"* was not a derogatory one but merely a state of fact. That it may have meant something similar to civilian in terms of spirituality as many of the Roman elite had called themselves *"Miles Christi"* (Soldiers of Christ).

C. Mohrmann suggested that it simply meant *"outsider."*

Today many see a pagan as someone who worships one of many earth-based religions. Still, the term is in use to denote polytheistic (those who believe in many deities) or pantheistic (those who believe that God is in everything, that God and the material world are one) and any non Judeo-Christian religion.

That being said, we must also look at the word neo-pagan. The majority of neo-pagans believe that paganism is an ancient form of worship that essentially died out and was not inherited in any substantial form. That neo-paganism is simply a new form of paganism, redefined, and reorganized. Hence the neo prefix. It hearkens back to the old ways without ever really being that old. Neo-pagans are also believed to be primarily monotheistic, in other words they believe in one energy, one God, but that this God form is indescribable, that for the sake of human understanding must be divided into two or more entities in representation of polarity, the male and female, the elements, etc. Not everyone within the pagan community agrees, some do claim to be pure polytheists.

Now, Paleopaganism, is simply used to refer to polytheistic tribal faiths such as Buddhism, Shinto and Hinduism. These are original, non-Abrahamic faiths brought down through generations, seemingly unchanged since the pre-Christian era.

So all in all I've written a lot here on paganism but it all comes down to one thing, paganism in whichever form as you understand it, is merely a broad term for any non-Abrahamic belief system. Prior to the mid-twentieth century, even atheists and agnostics claimed to pagan then with the movement that slowly died out. Now rarely do we hear of a pagan atheist.

Wicca

Okay, so just for a minute let us continue on this idea of Neo-paganism and the belief that there are no true ties between the ancient religions and the "new" ancient religions save for the deities and Sabbats. So Wicca or WICA, as Gardener called it, would be a completely new religion. Upon talking to a few wiccans, I soon realized their point of view which was that many wiccans do not even cast spells or call themselves witches. They are merely on a spiritual path that involves the Sabbats, Esbats, and Lord and Lady, as well as other constructs similar to what our understanding of witchcraft would be. The difference is in the spell casting, although that is an aspect of the religion that many wiccans end up being drawn to. In essence, many wiccans believe that Wicca is the religion and Witchcraft is the practice. To many wiccans, theirs is a spiritual practice like Islam, Judaism, Catholicism, etc., and Witchcraft is to wiccans as prayer is to Catholics; it is a practice that happens within the religion. Catholics don't have to pray just as Wiccans don't have to cast spells. Wiccans also believe that because witchcraft is a practice, it can be combined with any religion.

A close up of a witch's altar during a Mabon ritual.

One very modern Wiccan, who is known throughout cyberspace as Silver Lotus, wrote a wonderful view on her blog (which can be found in the resources) *The Lotus Pond* discussing the exact differences as she sees them. Her view is consistent with many in the Wiccan community and she has been kind enough to allow me to share:

Wicca and Witchcraft: The Differences

The difference between Wicca and Witchcraft can be summarized simply: Wicca is a religion whereas Witchcraft is a practise. That begs the questions of what is a religion and what is a practise.

A religion is a spiritual belief system, such as Christianity, Islam, or Wicca. It is a series of beliefs, based around observance to or worship of deities and/or spirits. A practise is something that is done, such as prayer, meditation, or magic. Simply put, magic is a practise and Paganism is a religion. Wicca is a subset of Paganism, and magic/spell casting is the main goal of Witchcraft.

It is, of course, possible to practise magic without being a Witch. There are other forms, such as Ceremonial Magic. And magic can also be part of a religion—some argue that prayer is a version of magic, and that the Wiccan Circle is enacted prayer.

The main difference between Wicca and Witchcraft come with the differences in intent. The purpose of Wicca is to honour the Lord and Lady, observe the turns of the Wheel of the Year, and to pay attention to one's spirituality. Wicca is intimately tied to one's relationship with the divine, by whatever faces They choose to show to us. Witchcraft, on the other hand, **does not** have to involve deities. Instead, it is concerned with the use of spells and herbs to achieve a desired end–healing, love, protection, etc.

Because Witchcraft is a practise and not a religion, it is possible to be a member of just about any religion and also be a Witch. (Of course, different religions have different opinions about the morals of being a Witch, but that is neither here nor there.) The openness of Wiccans and other Pagans toward magic and the unexplained makes it all the more likely that these people will be drawn to Witchcraft. But be aware that not all Wiccans are Witches. Many do not cast spells of any type. Instead, they focus solely on their relationship with the divine and on their quest for spirituality.

There are some Witches who will say that Witchcraft is also their religion. And I am no position to argue with them. But I would like to point out that it is possible to cast a spell without calling upon a deity. (Instead, one focuses the power within themselves or within nature.) There are also Wiccans who claim that all Wiccans are Witches. Here, I am able to argue. I am Wiccan, but I am not a Witch. I do not cast spells, work magic, or work with herbs. My focus is on the divine and my spirituality. Although I will admit to being interested in exploring certain aspects of Witchcraft, and can perhaps see myself heading down that path in the near future. But Witchcraft will only be an adjunct to my fulfilling spiritual path.

It is easy to become confused about the differences between Wicca and Witchcraft. Many books aimed at beginners tend to use the terms Wiccan and Witch interchangeably, and focus just as much on religious holidays (such as Sabbats) as they do on magic and spells. I suspect that this is because many Wiccans eventually find themselves drawn to Witch-craft. Personally, though, I would rather see books for beginners focusing more on the basic of the Wiccan faith, and leaving the exploration of Witchcraft for a later time, if the one decides to peruse that path.

Remember, Wicca is a religion and Witchcraft is a practice. Not all Witches are Wiccan, nor are all Wiccans Witches. The focus of Wicca is on the Lord and Lady, the Wheel of the Year, and one's spirituality. The focus of Witchcraft is on the casting of spells (magic) and the use of herbs towards a specific end or goal.

Silver Lotus is from Canada and started working within the Wiccan faith at the age of sixteen. At thirty-one she is a proud Wiccan with a penchant for cross stitch and a meticulous manner.

As I said earlier, her views are shared by many within the Wiccan community, on-line, off-line, in covens and solitaries.

A witch's altar.

Witchcraft

When it came to the subject of witchcraft, I had to go to the source, as I knew it. Laurie Cabot, founder of the Cabot clan and system of magick.

> Witchcraft is a religion, we do not practice naturism like Wiccans do, Gardner brought naturism, just like Sanders brought the Great Rite.
>
> We will invoke our Gods and Goddesses and allow them to speak through us. Our Gods and Goddesses were alive in this world they were alive they lived in a higher level of magick in their day, that we do not do any longer. If you call on Rhiannon, for instance, she was deceived and self-deceived and she used her magick in such weird ways, you know, today we would have stopped all that. She didn't she went along with things and then used her magick to run faster than wind, to do this or to do that. But now we call on her like a Catholic would call on a saint. We call them in and say 'Ok Rhiannon, don't let me be deceived again. Please let me learn how to not be self-deceiving.' That's how we talk to our Goddess. The word witch is not an umbrella term for magick in Africa or magick in different cultures, those are different cultures and they have their own words. It has been used as an umbrella word for too long.

I decided that maybe looking a little deeper into the actual etymology of both the words *Wicca* and *Witchcraft* might help to shed a little light on the debate between the two.

Wicca: The True Meaning

Wicca derives from an old English word which is the male version of *wicce* meaning "male witch, soothsayer, magician." The word *Wicca* was used for the first time in the religious context by Gerald Gardner in his *Witchcraft Today,* a book he published in 1954. He established Wica (no that is not a misspelling) as a religious tradition with its base being in the practice of witchcraft. So technically, when someone uses the word *Wicca* or *Wica* they are actually referring to Gerald Gardner's tradition.

Is Witchcraft A Religion?

On the other hand, witchcraft is derived from the old English word *wiccecraft* which describes the practices and beliefs held by the *wicce*. Some early documentation of the wicce comes to us from around 1480 and discusses the negative feelings against the wicce. Some believe this document to be a precursor of the burning times and anti-witch movement that happened later in the 16th, 17th, and 18th centuries. Magick, which many Wiccans believe to be the equivalent of prayer and complete separate from Wicca, is the science of energy manipulation, inherent in the practices of witchcraft. Old English *wicca* means "female sorceress or magician." The word *witch* has evolved to mean a man or woman who practices witchcraft. The label of "witch" has also developed to denote "one who incorporates magick and religion" instead of someone who only practices magick.

So is Witchcraft a religion? Yes, I think we can say it is, but we can also say that Wicca is a branch of the Witchcraft religion and that paganism is the umbrella term for any earth-focused or non-Judeo-Christian religion. One wonderful quote comes from SpringWolf's ThePaganPath.com. It says:

> Today modern Traditions are based on advancements in science, merging practices from two or more traditions into one, or even taking aspects of beliefs from other religions and merging them with neo-pagan traditions to create new traditions of the religion.
>
> Through all this, there is one constant – Witchcraft is the religion that sets the foundation of belief and the Traditions further define and implement those beliefs into their own perspectives of practice. Defining their own creed, troth, or rede of faith to provide guidance and principles for that tradition. Wicca is a tradition of Witchcraft, along with a large number of other Traditions that existed before the creation of Wicca.

Our Mothers of the Craft

I have never made a big issue of my own family's long involvement in witchcraft, but today the 'in' thing is to lay claim to being a hereditary witch; this is again divided into the idea that, being a matriarchal religion, it must also—in some cases—be a sort of psychic women's liberation movement. In reality, witches respect only the Life Force, and this is related to polarity, one of the basic laws of the universe.

~ Sybil Leek

Today, throughout the Witchcraft community there are many wonderful teachers and individuals who practice the many different branches of the craft and are activists for witches' rights.

However, right now I would like to talk about those teachers who have come before us and those who are still living—those who have introduced different teachings of the craft into our society, sacrificed their time, energy and voices to make way for the next generation of witches. This is a sacrifice, which seems to sometimes sadly be forgotten

by some of us in today's mainstream and witch community. Without some of these women of the old religion, we might never be where we are today within the world of witchcraft. This chapter will cover those women who in my heart and our history, made a difference and have paved a path of freedom and enlightenment for other witches to live open and freely as modern witches.

Sybil Leek

First To Bring Witchcraft to the United States

Member of One of the Four Original New Forest Covens

All human beings have magic in them. The secret is to know how to use this magic, and astrology is a vital tool for doing just that...

~Sybil Leek
Book of Fortune Telling, 1969

Sybil Leek was such a fascinating woman, witch, astrologer, psychic, gypsy, and author in her time. She became Britain's most famous English witch and wrote more than sixty books throughout her life on many areas of the occult. On February 22, 1917 Sybil Leek was born into the world. (During my search, I found several different years which say Sybil's birth year was 1922 and 1923. I shall go with the most common year, I could find.) But was the world ready for such a person? She grew up in the village of Normacot, Staffordshire, England, with her parents and grandmother; each family member playing an important role with her development into the arts of witchcraft and astrology. Her father would teach her all about herbs and the magical properties each contained, and taught her about working alongside nature and animals. Her grandmother taught her about the esoteric, astrology, and all the astrological signs and symbols. Her family without any known reason (to my knowledge and research) decided it be in the best interest to home school Sybil; who at the time only received three years of an orthodox school education.

While still being very young, around nine years old, a close family friend by the name of Aleister Crowley would come and visit. Aleister, became fond of Sybil and would discuss witchcraft and read his own

WITCHES RIDE AGAIN

February 20th 1964

High Priestess and a jackdaw

DAILY TELEGRAPH REPORTER

A BATTLE of witches was joined at University College, London, last night when modern British witches turned up to a Folklore Society lecture. The lecturer, Dr. Rossell Hope Robbins, was out to prove that witches did not exist and never had.

Every time he said anything like that Mr. Hotfoot Jackson, a forest jackdaw, squawked loudly. He was sitting on the shoulder of Mrs. Sybil Leek, 41, High Priestess of British Witchcraft.

Mrs. Leek has been a witch since childhood. " I was always conscious of trance conditions," she said to me. " I found it useful in maths lessons."

No, she did not ride on a broomstick. " That's just a phallic symbol," she explained. She didn't believe in God, but felt responsible to the Supreme Being.

Coven meetings

Her coven met four times a year at midnight on the Red Sabbats. " These are religious meetings at which we renew our energies," she said. " The power of renewal comes from the Supreme Being."

Dr. Robbins, an American born in Cheshire, was introduced as an early example of the brain drain. He certainly drained mine and I began to wish I had not been in a trance condition at shorthand lessons.

He kept saying words like demonology, heresy, theological twist, but witch was witch I cannot tell. Now and again he hit out plainly and Mr. Hotfoot Jackson hooted.

Witches and warlocks were on the warpath after the lecture about Dr. Robbins's retort to a question from Mrs. Leek.

" Do you really not believe that there are all over the world to-day group of people sincerely practising the old religion?" she asked.

" I am not interested in sincerity." Dr. Robbins replied.

Two bessom broomsticks were found chained to a bench in the quadrangle outside the hall. Mrs. Leek dismissed them as a students' jape, unworthy of modern witchery and left for a night out touring the sights of London in a car.

Mrs. Sybil Leek, the High Priestess of British witchcraft, with Mr. Hotfoot Jackson, a forest jackdaw, sitting on her shoulder, at the Folklore Society lecture at University College last night. British witches turned up at the lecture at which Dr. Rossell Hope Robbins was out to prove that witches did not exist.

An article in the *Daily Telegraph* 1964. Sybil turned up to a debate at University College, London, about witches. *Courtesy of Melissa Harrington and Melissa Seims.*

poetry to her during his visits with the Leek family. Because of his encouragement to write, Sybil, still a young teenager, had published her first poetry book. In Sybil's book, *Diary of a Witch*, she talks about some of her experiences; one in particularly really seemed to stand out for me. It goes as follows:

> One day Crowley cupped my face in his hands and spoke to my grandmother.
> "This is the one who will take up where I leave off," he said, for once gentle and serious at the same time. "You'd better remember that, young lady. You'll hear all sorts of things said about me and they'll say the same things about you, but I shall have broken the ground for you."
> He turned to my grandmother.
> "She is the one who will survive. She'll live to see occultism almost being understood. That will be the day, won't it, old lady?"

A few more years passed by and Sybil met a concert pianist who was around twenty-four years older than she was and he became her music teacher. She was only sixteen but fell madly in love and decided to marry him. This was a rather short marriage, for he died two years later. (During my research on Sybil Leek, I could not find the name of her first husband; or just how and why he had passed away.) Heartbroken with sorrow and grief, Sybil returned home to her grandmother's house. Shortly after Sybil had settled in, she was needed at a coven in George Du Loup, a small community in the South of France near Nice.

There Sybil needed to be initiated and to replace her elderly aunt's position as high priestess. From working in this coven, the New Forest covens in England were born.

During the Second World War, Sybil decided to join the London's Red Cross and became a nurse at a military hospital in Netley. At this hospital, she worked on the ward for the prisoners of war because she could speak French and some of the German language.

> It was a nerve-racking experience, dealing with prisoners of war who were sick, many of whom had lost a limb. The Germans were aggressive and rude to all the female staff. They were not truly interested in living, and many fought against medical attention. It was a great lesson in discipline to nurse the enemy and know he was still the enemy. We were told that we must not, under any circumstances, allow a prisoner to provoke us. In theory, it was fine; in practice, very

hard. We were all high-spirited girls from good families, and every one of us had men from the family in the service. We had to withstand barrages of abuse, physical onslaught, and sexual advances, and we still had to try to be pleasant.

~Sybil Leek
My Life in Astrology, 1972

When the war finally ended, Sybil moved to a small town called Burley to start her life once more. She soon became friends with the local gypsies and lived among them for some time, learning the traditions and their magical ways of living. Being born into a magical family, Sybil had the witch's blood running through her veins, which allowed her to join their coven called Horsa and she became a high priestess for a short time. At some point, Sybil decided to leave the life of the gypsies and open an antique shop in Burley, which soon became very successful.

When word spread that a psychic-witch had opened a shop in Burley, tourists and media flocked to the antique store – although there was never one true occult item to be found there. Except of course for Sybil herself. Unfortunately, her antique business was suffering from lack of sales and even the property owner who leased the shop to Sybil was about to send another blow to her business. Witchcraft seemed to still be looked down upon and not very accepted with the locals, especially Sybil's property owner who refused to renew Sybil's lease to her shop. Even though tourist brought money into Burley, the locals did not like the constant traffic coming and going or the media asking questions and taking pictures.

In 1963, Sybil proclaimed that she wanted to open up a witch school in Britain in the *World News Reporter.* She talked about leaving the beamed cottage and looking for a big, rambling house with *"the right atmosphere."* Sybil talked about the letters that she got from around the world, people looking to her to cure ailments, find love, and get money. Most, she said, were addressed to *"The Witch, England"* or *"The Witch, New Forest."* Sybil says something that I feel rings true for many people today in modern witchcraft. *"Occult forces are quite neutral. It rests with the individual how they are used. The same force can be used for Black Magic or white witchcraft."*

Almost every newspaper article starts out by talking about the crow on her shoulder; a beautiful companion to Sybil, his name was Mr. Hotfoot Jackson. She kept Hotfoot because of her heritage and one woman in particular: Molly Leigh whom Sybil was descended from and greatly inspired by. Sybil's ancestor was an interesting character, known

'Witch' plans school for sorcerers

October 20th, 1963.

NEWS OF THE WORLD REPORTER

BRITAIN'S No. 1 Witch, huddled in a cloak, with a jackdaw perched on her shoulder, sat beside her cast-iron cauldron yesterday and talked of her plan to start a school for witches.

Sybil Leek, 41-year-old mother of two schoolboys, wants to move out of her beamed cottage in the New Forest village of Burley and find a big, rambling, lonely old house with "the right atmosphere."

Then she will invite students of witchcraft to study and take part in magic circle activities. Scores of people want to learn from the witch of the New Forest. She has even had letters from African witch doctors.

Other letters have arrived from New Zealand, Australia, Italy, France and Germany.

Most plead with her to cure illnesses, or settle rows. Some are simply addressed to "The Witch, England," or "The Witch, New Forest."

CRANKS

A lot are cranks who think she can help them make fortunes or sort out love problems, says Sybil.

In the old world village of Burley some people laugh and jeer. They call out behind her as she climbs the hill to carry out rites in the forest.

"Old witch, old mother witch," jeer the teenagers.

Many people in the district advise visitors who ask about Sybil to have nothing to do with her.

That is my advice, too. Steer clear of this mumbo-jumbo.

Sybil believes that the occult philosophy for which witches were once hanged invests a person with enough power to control the world.

Occult forces are quite neutral, she says. It rests with the individual how they are used. The same force can be used for Black Magic or for white witchcraft.

Sybil, the witch, at work on a ritual in her sorcery room

An article from *News of the World* 1963 about a witch school that Sybil Leek wanted to establish. *Courtesy of Melissa Harrington and Melissa Seims.*

for her own blackbird, which sat on her shoulder—she was very much an eccentric loner. She would deliver dairy to the village.

Reverend Spencer was the first to accuse Molly of witchcraft; he claimed that her bird sat upon the local pubs sign and that it turned the beer stale. After her death, they actually exhumed her body at the behest of Spencer and couple of other clerics and then threw her blackbird into the coffin, essentially suffocating him and killing him. They then reburied Molly North to South at a right angle from all of the others buried in the cemetery. Sybil went to visit her ancestor multiple times and I think, she looked upon Molly as a guide of sorts.

In 1964, Sybil started working with the Witches Research Association; an article was written about it in the *Daily Herald*. In it she talks about her aspirations to have an office in London, a monthly magazine called *Witchcraft Today* and felt that part of the aim was to improve the witches public image. Unfortunately, Sybil's presidency did not last very long, after being evicted from her home, she decided to go to America.

Sybil knew her work was not over yet and decided to accept an offer from the American Publishing House in 1964 to come to the United States for a visit and talk about her new antique book called *A Shop in the High Street*. When Sybil's plane touched down in New York, she soon became surrounded by media reporters and started giving many interviews after that. Soon after, Sybil settled in New York as a resident of the United States.

THAT TAKES YOU OFF THE BEATEN TRACK

Broomstick, jackdaw and a cauldron by the door.: Mrs. Leek admits there's witchery afoot.

PICTURE BY CHRIS BARHAM

the right place at the right time.

Mrs. Leek walks up to 15 miles—it's classy to take your car. She also carries the cauldron (it always seems to be her turn to carry the cauldron) and has never yet got her thought-transferences muddled and gone to the wrong place.

The New Forest is, of course, ideal for witches.

Invocation

But covens do meet in much more prosaic surroundings. Mrs. Leek told me of a coven which meets in the living room of a flat in Brighton.

She went there once and the witches played a record of "genuine voodoo music" and the floor burst into flames. The witches discovered later that this particular record was an invocation to the God of Fire.

Her family react surprisingly quietly. Her husband, Brian, who has a beard and an expression of quiet resignation, said simply: "Look at it this way—I'd rather have her on my side than against me."

Her 12-year-old son Julian drew a crayon picture last week. It showed a witch crouching over a cauldron in the forest. The caption was: "Mummy at work."

But though you might giggle a bit, it is as well not to take liberties with Mrs. Leek. She made it fairly clear to me that she expected this to be a reasonable article.

"As you may know," she said, "we have this system of sticking pins in effigies of people we might want to get at. Sandstone and spit make the best effigies. . ."

An article about Sybil that appeared in the *Daily Herald* September 16, 1963. *Courtesy of Melissa Harrington and Melissa Seims.*

Her new black magic has USA spellbound

Dec. 13th, 1969.

Former New Forest resident Sybil Leek has just written a best-seller in America, called Diary of a Witch. So Sybil, now known as " the Californian seeress," is cashing in on the craze for witchcraft and the study of the occult now raging over there.

In fact, Sybil was in the running for an official post as county witch, but was beaten by a broom stick by so-called " sixth-generation witch " Mrs. Louise Huebner, who has just been appointed by the Los Angeles entertainments board.

Much of the interest in witchcraft arose from the investigations into the black arts by film producer Roman Polanski, whose wife, Sharon Tate, was murdered recently.

Sybil (pictured), who lived at Ringwood and Burley, first became interested in witchcraft in the New Forest, about which district she wrote several books before leaving for America two years ago.

An article about Sybil from 1969 (article source unknown). *Courtesy of Melissa Harrington and Melissa Seims.*

The shop which Sybil Leek owned during the 1950s, shown as it looks today in Burley. *Photo courtesy of Gillian Moy.*

A man named Hans Holzer, who was a parapsychologist contacted her. He asked Sybil to join him on a few investigations of haunted places and was interested in her abilities as a psychic. She agreed and these opportunities with Hans Holzer lead her to do many television and radio appearances. This was a huge stepping-stone and opened the doors for those psychics and witches of today who work in the paranormal field.

Not liking the New York weather very much, Sybil decided to move to Los Angeles where she met a man by the name of Dr. Israel Regardie. He was an authority on the subject of Kabbalah and ritual magic; together the two studied, talked, and practiced the Golden Dawn rituals.

Years later, Sybil moved to Florida and continued to promote the positive benefits and spirituality of the old religion; during that time she also became known as a great astrologer. Sybil toured all over the States and outside the United States giving lectures on a variety of subjects such as reincarnation.

Sybil did have a mouth on her and was never afraid to use it, especially with other witches and while talking about her own beliefs. With her pet crow upon her shoulder and even sometimes a boa constrictor wrapped around her neck, she spoke from the heart and strongly believed in the act of cursing.

She did not believe in the act of nudity in the covens during the rituals and disproved of the act of taking drugs. Sybil was big into the environmental issues and was one of the first modern witches to bring these concerns to the public. She was also very matriarchal in her thinking but made no part of the Feminist movement.

At the age of sixty-five years, Sybil lost her nine-month battle with cancer on October 26, 1982. It's sad, but I feel that many people have forgotten about Sybil Leek. When I speak with some witches, it's as if Gerald, Doreen, Ray Buckland, and Scott Cunningham were the big players. But Sybil had her role too. She was one of the first to bring witchcraft to the United States, one of the first kitchen witches to publish a book (see *Diary of a Witch,* page 86. She talks about her grandmother's athalme—no, that is not a spelling error). In addition, she was the first to publish a book regarding the theological aspects of witchcraft. Overall, she was not a woman to mess with.

Doreen Valiente

Mother of Modern Witchcraft

Established the Witches Research Association

Let My worship be in the heart that rejoices, for behold, all acts of love and pleasure are My rituals.

~Doreen Valiente

Commonly regarded as the "Mother of Modern Witchcraft," Doreen Valiente was born Doreeen Dominy, in South London in 1922. Her parents were both devout Christians but early on Doreen felt an affinity for other religions. She used to play by herself running up and down the streets riding a broomstick—Doreen didn't seem to notice at the time the act she was portraying. Her parents did though, and quickly admonished her for her behavior; being strict Christians, their biggest fear was that one day Doreen would indeed become a witch. A prophecy that would be fulfilled later in Doreen's life, by the age of thirteen, Doreen was already practicing the use of "simple magick." She even did some of her "simple magick" for her mother who constantly complained about their housekeeper. This woman, Doreen's mother asserted, had been harassing her. Doreen was not about to let it go any further and told her mother to bring her some of the woman's hair. She created a poppet for her mother using a doll, the woman's hair, and some traditional herbs. Doreen cast a spell. Shortly thereafter, a blackbird began harassing the woman who was harassing Doreen's mother!

Doreen also says that the harassment stopped completely after the spell ran its course. At fifteen, Doreen was attending a convent school; finally, she had enough and walked out, refusing to return.

Doreen Meets Gerald Gardner

At the age of thirty, Doreen was initiated into Gerald Gardner's coven in New Forest, through a mutual friend named "Dafo." This woman used an alias, because only the year before practitioners of witchcraft could still be persecuted. Dafo introduced Doreen to Gardner and immediately the two struck a friendship; and in 1953, she received her initiation. Gardner initiated her himself, given that the law according to Wica was that one of the opposite sex must conduct the ritual. He gave her the rights on Midsummer's Eve.

Whilst studying under Gardner, Doreen noticed some indiscrepancies in his *Book of Shadows* which he claimed to be completely original and from the New Forest coven. Some of the work came from Crowley, particularly some of the Mass, which Gardner often read. This irked Doreen and so she brought it up to Gardner. She believed that the bulk of the work was most likely original, but that somehow it had been fragmented and so he had filled it in, taking inspiration from Masonic teachings, Crowley, and other occult influences. Gardner challenged her, asking if she thought she could do better. Doreen was never one to back down from her truths. She accepted the challenge, taking out the occult influences and adding her own words—she essentially created what we know today as Wica.

Doreen grew angry with Gardner as he loved the lime light and she shunned the publicity as much as possible. She felt that he was not keeping the tenets of the Old Religion and its secretive ways and that he was dishonoring it by drawing so much attention to himself. She proposed the institution of a new law within the system, which would not allow any of the witches within their religious sect to speak to the press unless given permission by the Elders. Gardner, herself, and anyone would have to hold to this same tenet. Gardner had a hissy fit around it and presented her with a copy of the Old Laws that Doreen did not believe to be an accurate example of the true old law but merely something whipped up by Gardener so he could have his cake and eat it too.

The statue of the Horned God and Mother Goddess of Wicca, owned by Doreen Valiente, and crafted by Bel Bucca. *Picture courtesy of Midnightblueowl.*

Doreen and the Witchcraft Research Association

After that, Doreen severed her connection with Gardner completely. Before her mentor's death in 1964, they would restore friendship, but it would never be the same. During that same year, Doreen also lost her mother and was initiated in the Cochrane Tradition of witchcraft. She also took up presidency of the Witchcraft Research Association. Initially established by Gerard Noel, Sybil Leek sat in the President's chair until she was forced to leave the U.K. after being persecuted and evicted from her home.

In an interview with the *Evening Argus* that centers on the W.R.A. and Valiente as its president, she discusses the reasons for its existence stating:

A perfectly serious association. Our aim is impartial research into the old traditions of Witchcraft. We are just a body of people who have set out honestly and sincerely to study a very fascinating subject.

The association also produced a magazine called *Pentagram* which sold for about two shillings; its first copy went out in July of 1964. The

"Letter From The Editor" Doreen wrote:

LETTER OF WELCOME FROM DOREEN VALIENTE
The Editor, BRIGHTON *Pentagram*
July 9th, 1964
BM/Eleusis, London, W.C.

Dear Sir,

I am glad to have this opportunity of welcoming the first issue of the *Pentagram*. It is a curious coincidence that 1964 is just thirteen years after the repeal of the last of the Witchcraft Acts in this country, which took place in 1951.

Ever since that date, the old Craft of the Wise has steadily progressed towards recognition as a genuine religious tradition. Nor is it merely a relic of the past; it has significance for people of the present day, disillusioned as they often are with more orthodox creeds, and "orphaned of the great Mother," Nature, by the stresses of modern life.

Like every live movement, there are differing opinions among us – and a good thing, too. From brainwashed uniformity, may we long be preserved!

Owing to the years of persecution, the old traditions have become fragmented, with one coven or group of covens preserving certain aspects of the old beliefs, that have been handed down to them, while others retain and place emphasis upon other aspects.

I think we should take this face into account, and recognize that no section of the cult has the right to say, "We and we alone, are the genuine article; anyone who is different from us is wrong." Rather, we should respect each other's views, when sincerely held, whether or not we agree with them.

If we are willing to do this, then the way will be open for a truly great work to be performed; namely, the piecing together again of all the true parts of the ancient tradition, to make a coherent whole so meaningful in all it's potentialities that it at once command the respect of intelligent and thoughtful people.

I hope the W.R.A. may be able to help in this aspiration, by acting as a kind of United nations of the Craft. I hope it will promote research, and the recording of traditions that might otherwise be lost; and I hope also that it will work for mutual understand and unity of purpose, that will make such research possible.

Goodluck, and "Blessed Be…"

Doeen Valiente

Even though thirteen years had passed, there was still a low tolerance for any practitioners of witchcraft. In the first issue a reader asks why, when being interviewed or contacted, witches mainly use P. O. boxes. Here is the response:

The answer is simple. One prolific interview-giver has been evicted from a shop and two homes. A London Witch was evicted from her flat last year following certain press reports. The days of victimization are certainly not dead yet!

Nearer "home," a mischief-maker who discovered the actual whereabouts of the principal sponsor of the WRA attempted to "extort money by menaces"– as the lawyers say.

Prior to the death of Gardner and Doreen's mom, the main reason she didn't like giving interviews and being completely "out of the broomcloset" was that her parents didn't know. It was the culmination of their worst fears, but in light of the atrocities being committed against witches everywhere in the country, Doreen felt the call to stand up for her brothers and

12—EVENING ARGUS, TUESDAY, SEPTEMBER 29, 1964

Now the witches

Brighton witch Miss Doreen Valiente with some of the tools of her "trade."

have their own 'trade union'

ITS name is almost staid—the Witchcraft Research Association. Even Magic Circle sounds exotic beside it. But its aim is to delve into the history and practices of a subject which some say is vile. Others mildly amusing . . .

THEY FORM A RESEARCH ASSOCIATION

A COVEN

MAGAZINE

An article about Doreen's involvement with the Witchcraft Research Association, formed in 1964. *Courtesy of Melissa Harrington and Melissa Seims.*

have their own 'trade union'

ITS name is almost staid—the Witchcraft Research Association. Even Magic Circle sounds exotic beside it. But its aim is to delve into the history and practices of a subject which s o m e say is vile. Others mildly amusing . . .

The association was formed earlier this year and has still to hold its first meeting. But, predictably enough, it has links with Brighton—in a basement flat in Lewes Crescent on the seafront.

There lives Doreen Valiente, one of Britain's few witches—self-styled, of course, since there is no university degree in the subject—a mild, early-middle-aged woman with a West Country burr and one passionate hobby: the old religion.

She is a member of the W.R.A.; she refers to it by its initials. It is, she says, "a perfectly serious association. Our aim is impartial research into the old traditions of witchcraft. We are just a body of people who have set out honestly and sincerely to study a very fascinating subject."

A COVEN

The association, she agrees, has yet to meet. But it has been active. In its six or so months of existence, Miss Valiente says it has:

● Discovered a c o v e n of witches not known before to other active witches. She would not say where it is.

● Collected a number of spells and invocations not before known. As they were given in confidence she could not say anything about them.

● Acquired a small quantity of an English incense made by a witch to a witch's brew. It was given to Miss Valiente in a small red cardboard carton marked "Viscount de-mothing crystals."

MAGAZINE

"It is genuine English witch's incense," the Lewes Crescent witch said as she burned a little in a brass incense burner. "I'll have to try to get the recipe."

The witch who made the incense also showed Miss Valiente an unguent which she claimed

THEY FORM A RESEARCH ASSOCIATION

helped in clairvoyance. Miss Valiente is after a sample of that too.

The association has produced one issue of a four-page magazine about witchcraft. It sold for 2s. Another is due.

Miss Valiente, who is proud of her claim to be a witch, is pleased with the progress of the association so far. "People are very cautious about giving information about witchcraft to anyone because there has been so much of the wrong sort of publicity," she said.

She estimates that she is one of only a hundred or so witches in this country, but she says that many people have information about the old religion which the W.R.A. would like to collect.

So, although the association has not yet attained substance, she says it has a great future. She

would like to see it open an office in London, a library, hold m e e t i n g s, trace relics for meetings. It is interested in anything pagan, superstitious, occult, folk, traditional.

And it wants to combat inaccurate statements about witchcraft. For instance, said Miss Valiente, that witches dance in the nude. "Some did," she said, "but others think that nudity actually detracts from a witch's power.

"And, anyway," she added, "can you imagine what it must be like meeting and dancing in the nude in this country in a normal summer!"

Enlargements of photo at left. *Courtesy of Melissa Harrington and Melissa Seims.*

sisters. At the first inaugural meeting of the WRA held in the Hotel Rubens on October 3rd, fifty people were present, as reported by Justine Glass, an attendee and writer for *Prediction* magazine.

There, Doreen made a grand speech regarding the unity of the covens and how already the WRA had found a coven that had as yet been undiscovered, an unguent that was to aid in clairvoyance as well as real english witches incense. She also spoke on the misconceptions of witchcraft, as probably half of the people present were not of the faith; she described the Horned God and his label of Satan, among other things. She ended by speaking the words of the Wiccan Rede specifically that last couple of lines: *"An ye harm none, do as ye will. Merry meet…merry part."*

No photographs were allowed to be taken during the dinner and lecture that followed, but I am sure each of the attendees can probably remember in vivid detail exactly what happened. I know if I had been there I surely would have.

An article by Helen Galley in the Brighton *Evening Argus*, April 25, 1984. *Courtesy of Melissa Harrington and Melissa Seims.*

Doreen Valiente and Cochran's Witchcraft

Doreen really did find a middle ground when it came to being out in the media maintaining a certain form of anonymity. The Cochrane coven that she belonged to, its laws and system of magick only aided in cementing her beliefs in keeping witchcraft out of the spotlight as religion and maintaining its secrets. Cochrane started his coven, The Clan of Tubal Cain, around the same time as Gardner. It eventually became known as the "1734" tradition. He explains his reasoning behind the grouping of numbers (not a date) to Joe Wilson, a witch in America who he began to teach. You can read a portion of the letter below concerning one of the puzzles relating to 1734:

> The order of 1734 is not a date of an event, but a grouping of numerals that mean something to a witch. One that becomes seven states of wisdom is the Goddess of the Cauldron. Three that are the Queens of the Elements, fire belonging to Man alone and the Black-smith God. Four are Queens of the Wind Gods. The Jewish orthodoxy believe that whomever knows the Holy and Unspeakable name of God has absolute power over the world of form. Very briefly the Name of

DOREEN'S GUIDE TO THE COVENS

Brighton Evening argus, March 1st, 1972.

A 'Which?' on the witches

SHAKESPEARE is much to blame for giving us a picture of witches as secret, black and midnight hags, hovering through the fog and filthy air.

Mrs Doreen Valiente, right, of Sillwood Place, Brighton, who calls herself a practising witch, is not like that at all. In fact she would have to disguise herself heavily before she could play in the witches' scenes in Macbeth.

An elder in the witchcraft movement, she is the author of what promises to be a startling book, An ABC of Witchcraft Past and Present, which Robert Hale and Company are to publish in June. It will be an impressive, illustrated volume of 416 pages, at £3.50.

In their preliminary notice, the publishers say : "This is the only book of its kind written by a practising witch. It is intended as not merely a history, but a guide to the many strange byways of a vast and fascinating subject."

Mrs Valiente would not thank anyone calling her a "white witch" : she prefers to be just a witch. Any division of witches into white and evil categories is not justified by history, she says.

AWARENESS

Her book will show that witchcraft is as old as the human race and its devotees as worshippers in the oldest religion of the world. They were pagan nature worshippers long before the Druids.

"Witchcraft is a philosophy and a way of life," she told a reporter. "It brings about a better enjoyment of living, a greater awareness of the beauties of the world."

Interest in witchcraft and in the occult generally, she says, has grown tremendously in recent years. This coincides with the coming in of the Aquarian Age when great changes are taking place.

Sussex, like other parts of the country, has several covens of witches who hold regular sabbats, with all the traditional ritual of dances, spells and sacrifices.

But, according to Mrs Valiente, they are merely play-acting and are regarded by real witches as something of a joke.

She firmly dissociates the genuine witches from the Satanists who, in Sussex and elsewhere, have often desecrated churches to celebrate the black mass.

"Genuine witches," she said, " see no necessity to dress up in the cast-off rags of Christianity. Witchcraft, as a religion, is far, far older than Christianity."

Born in London, Mrs Valiente comes of a family long associated with the New Forest, which she considers a mystic area.

With her Spanish-born husband, she has lived in Brighton since 1956, and her home contains many of the objects and charms historically associated with witchcraft and magic.

Apart from being an authority on witchcraft, she is a painter and a poet. Some of her poems have been read at the London meetings of the Poetry Society.

An article from the Brighton *Evening Argus* March 1, 1972. *Courtesy of Melissa Harrington and Melissa Seims.*

God spoken as Tetragrammaton ("I am that I am") breaks down in Hebrew to the letters IHVH, or the Adom Kadomon (The Heavenly Man). Adom Kadomon is a composite of all Archangels – in other words a poetic statement of the names of the Elements. So what the Jew and the Witch believe alike, is that the man who discovers the secret of the Elements controls the physical world. 1734 is the witch way of saying IHVH.

~Robert Cochrane

Due to this, there are now several Cochranian covens within the United States, but no two are alike; they hand down Cochrane's papers just as they do a *Book of Shadows* in other traditions. Slowly, Doreen began to watch as Cochrane became more controlling within the coven, openly having an affair with another member while his wife watched unable to do anything. His obsession with potions and brew that gave hallucinegenic benefits became out of control. He went after the Gardenarians, verbally attacking them at every opportunity. For Doreen having been with Gardner, this was very insulting.

Eventually, Doreen left the clan, becoming disillusioned much like she had been with Gardner. Cochrane had lost not just a good friend, but in a matter of months, his clan and marriage fell apart. With all of these weights upon his mind and increasing isolation, Cochrane sank into depression; the state of his mind is clearly seen when one reads the letter he wrote to Norman Gills sent in April of 1966:

> Many thanks for your letter, and the well-meant warning therein… I am now sans John – sans A.4, sans friends, and working by myself quite happily. It is surprising that the warning came the very week when the final and terribly painful blow fell. Old J. [Jane] is no mean psychic, since she warned me against little A. many months ago – and I took little or no heed. So I have learned. I am of course at the end of a phase – and being like yourself, a man without any true fate – except that which we shape ourselves – I would like to know where I go from here? Can you be a friend and have a look for me – for as you know, one cannot tell one's own future except by the merest glimpse, and I feel as if I am at the bottom of a well with little or no hope for the future. If you do decide to help me, then I would be very grateful if you would tell me the truth, and not cover up any blows.

During the first few months of 1966, Valiente found out through the grapevine that he was telling his followers of his plan to commit suicide on Midsummer. Valiente took the threats more seriously than others, even if they were empty as some proclaimed them to be. Cochrane sent the following to his student, Joe Wilson, in April of 1966, giving his version of the Witch Law:

> Witch Law: Do not do what you desire – do what is necessary. Take all you are given – give all of yourself. What I have – I hold. When all else is lost, and not until then, prepare to die with dignity.

He also wrote a letter to Norman Gills Bowers and William Gray who he counted as confidants, in this letter you can clearly see his suicidal intentions disguised as an old witch song:

> There you and I my loves
>
> There you and I will lie,
>
> When the cross of resurrection is broken,
>
> And our time has come to die,
>
> For no more is there weeping,
>
> For no more is there death,
>
> Only the golden sunset,
>
> Only the golden rest.

In Robert Cochrane's letter to Norman in March of 1966, a definitive show is given of Robert's suicidal plans:

> When the time comes pass this, and the other things which we have discussed, on to Mr. [Joe] Wilson, whom I am afraid I will not see.

At about the same time – April 1966 – he predicted in a letter to Wilson that the young American witch would be visiting Britain within a year.

Robert Cochrane went to the pub and met with the clan there, seemingly in good spirits and with healthy vigor. His attitude was deceptive, and the bulk of his people passed off his plans as merely a strike at getting back "in;" others saw it as a need for attention, and those who did take it seriously, such as Doreen, felt powerless.

Cochrane ended his life on the eve of the Summer Solstice in 1966, by ingesting nightshade. Some believe that it was an accident, that one of his experimental potions went horribly wrong; others believe it was just plain suicide. Yet those belonging to his coven believed, and still do, that it was an intended "male sacrifice" as often symbolically enacted during the Summer Solstice.

Not long after Midsummer, Doreen was coming home from a stay in the hospital, and she found a letter from Robert letting her know that by the time she actually got a chance to read the letter, he would be dead. She immediately got in touch with their mutual connections and found out that Cochrane had indeed committed suicide. Doreen Valiente went on to write a poem right after his death entitled: *Epitaph for a Witch*.

Epitaph for a Witch

To think that you are gone over the crest of the Hill.

As the Moon passed from her fulness, riding the Sky,

And the White Mare took you with her.

To think that we must wait another life

To drink wine from the Horns and leap the Fire.

Farewell from this world, but not the Circle.

That place that is between worlds

Shall hold return in due time. Nothing is lost.

The half of a fruit from the Tree of Avalon

Shall be our reminder among the fallen leaves

This life treads underfoot. Let the rain weep.

Waken in sunlight from the realms of sleep!

~Doreen Valiente

During Cochrane's inquest, the coroner had found a letter at the scene written by Robert's own hand seemingly after he took the poison. The coroner said he could only conclude that Robert had overdosed on Deadly Nightshade (belladonna) and Cochrane confirms that fact with his own letter:

> This is a carefully prepared suicide. This has been a mixture of Belladonna, Hellebore – terrible tasting stuff – and a dose of sleeping pills to counteract the movements, jerks, actions and all the rest, of my muscles caused by the high quantity of atropine in the Belladonna… This is to indicate, though that must be your opinion, that I took my own life while of sound mind.

BRITAIN'S BLACK MAGIC

San Francisco News, Dec. 7th, 1962.

Witches Are Riding High

By TOM A. CULLEN

BRIGHTON, Eng. (NEA) —Witchcraft is now enjoying its biggest boom in Britain since the Middle Ages.

Hundreds of men and women are now claiming to be witches and to have the power to heal or to cast spells. Some of these are genuine pagans.

Others are cranks or thrill-seekers, with a few out-and-out racketeers thrown in.

Witches and warlocks (as male witches are called) have been interviewed on television.

Witches in Cornwall, who specialize in curing warts and minor ailments, are said to be operating their own clinic along National Health Service lines.

Why the present interest in witches and black magic?

THE REVIVAL dates from 1951, when the last of Britain's anti-witch laws was repealed, according to Mrs. Doreen Valiente, an authority on witchcraft, whom I interviewed here in Brighton.

"Now witches are coming more and more into the open," she claims. "Their main trouble is finding premises. Ordinary apartments and houses are out, for witches like to make lots of noise."

At the same time Mrs. Valiente warned that some covens (witches' meeting places) are being run as rackets.

"Some of them attract members by promising exotic practices. Then the member is trapped into a compromising situation and afterwards blackmailed."

One Brighton coven is said to have charged American tourists large sums to witness so-called "Black Masses," and other rituals.

"MANY PEOPLE think that I, myself, am a witch," said dark-haired Mrs. Valiente, who has just completed a book on sorcery. Certainly, Mrs. Valiente's basement flat in Brighton contains one of the most amazing collections of witchcraft bric-a-brac to be found in the British Isles.

As for Mrs. Valiente, I noticed that she wie wearing a necklace of "witch stones," tiny fossils found on Brighton beach.

IN FACT, Mrs. Valiente has breathed the atmosphere of witchcraft from childhood, having been born in New Forest, Hampshire, a region noted for its sorcerers. "My family was notorious for their ability to commune with fairies," she said.

A favorite diversion of Sussex witches, according to legend, was to turn themselves into hares and run about the countryside at night.

Another specialty was known as the "Tanglewood Charm," a spell which caused people to wander out of their way and get lost.

"All of this may sound like nonsense," Mrs. Valiente conceded, "but how can one explain what happened to the group of teen-agers who visited Chanctonbury Ring recently?"

Chanctonbury Ring is the site of an old pagan temple on the Sussex Downs, and is ringed around with beech trees. Legend says that if one runs three times around the ring of trees at midnight and calls upon the Devil he will appear.

* * * *

"RECENTLY, some teen-agers decided to put the legend to a test.

"At first they contented themselves with doing the Twist and conventional rock 'n' roll. But, as midnight approached they danced more and more wildly around the ring invoking pagan powers.

"Suddenly an eerie silence descended upon the place followed by a feeling of terrible tension. It was as though one were being sucked up in the vacuum created by a nuclear explosion, as one of the teen-agers expressed it.

"Without consulting among themselves, they fled in panic down the hill. Today, nothing would induce those youngsters to go back to that spot," said Mrs. Valiente.

NEXT: A witch who answered a classified ad.

Tools of the trade—'Witch' displays black magic items

A *San Francisco News* article by Tom A. Cullen, December 7, 1962. *Courtesy of Melissa Harrington and Melissa Seims.*

Doreen was terribly stricken by the events, but just like the spiral dance, the world does keep turning and eventually Doreen would find herself on another quest. The WRA wrapped up in 1965, Cochrane being one of the writers, and his outspokenness against the Gardenarians growing louder arguments within their newsletter *Pentagram* began to happen consistently. But that wasn't that last of Doreen Valiente, not by a long shot.

Doreen's Legacy

In 1972, Doreen's husband passed away and she began to focus on her writing. During the seventies, she wrote the *ABC's of Witchcraft*, and

Natural Magic. These two books only added to her growing reputation as an expert in all things witchcraft and magick.

During the 1980s, because of Gardner's claims of being taught by a woman named "Old Dorothy Clutterbuck," Doreen decided to make it her mission to justify her friend and prove the existence of old Dorothy. This she did, eventually finding her birth certificate, as well as her death certificate.

Doreen passed away on September 1st, 1999. John, her heir, remained with her throughout. Even as the pains and cancer riddled her body, her mind remained sharp and her magick still powerful. Doreen wrote five books over the course of her life, each more impactful than the next. She attempted to unite the covens and break through old negative beliefs surrounding witchcraft. With her books, poetry, and presence, she guides the next generation of witches in the spiral dance. She is the Mother of Modern Witchcraft.

Laurie Cabot

Witch's Rights Activist

Created First Anti-Defamation League

"Certain things are everlasting. Magic is one of them."

~Laurie Cabot
Power of the Witch, 1989

I wish I had had the opportunity to do this with each of the foremothers and forefathers of Witchcraft. I love hearing stories from the source's mouth instead of relying on second-hand information. Laurie Cabot is best known for establishing the Cabot Tradition of witchcraft. Based in science, this tradition has spread like wildfire. Throughout the eighties and nineties, Laurie gained fame when she appeared on *Sally*, *Phil Donahue*, as well as documentaries and radio. You could not think of a witch without first thinking of Laurie Cabot. Now in the twenty-first century, many of our modern witches are forgetting their roots, forgetting the pains that our foremothers and fathers had to bear in order to bring freedom and recognition to the religion.

I was granted an interview with Laurie right before the rush of the October season hit Salem. I love metaphysical stores—there is a certain scent that wafts through the air, and in Laurie's store, you almost feel like you are in a library. It was bustling the day I went to see her, her staff all dressed in black, some with tattoos of crescent moons on their foreheads. They had opened a new section of the store called Tituba's House of Voodoo. There was so much to look at, it seemed like it was part store, part museum, and you could see Laurie's creative touch in everything.

Finally, the door opened to Laurie's office and there she was sitting behind a colorful desk surrounded by artwork and beautiful statuettes. Most, if not all, of the art she had done herself.

I have always remembered Laurie for her activism and that was what I wanted the focus to be during the interview. However, I realized early on, that this was not to be the average question and answer session I had expected. Whenever Laurie speaks, it is always in stories; at least it was during our interview. The stories and quotes (indented) are directly from the interview I had with Laurie, some are a little funny, others hair raising, but each are meaningful and full of information.

Becoming A Witch

Over the years, Laurie has openly discussed her training, as much as I love reading her books, it's very different from listening to her talk about it. I wanted to know about Laurie's history for two reasons; firstly, she is just such an interesting person, and secondly, upon preparation for this interview, I had read more than once on the web and heard from a couple of sites that they felt Laurie "made up" her religion. That she, much like Gerald Gardner, had no real basis or ties to any formal training that could be considered the true "old religion." I wanted to see what Laurie had to say about this.

People do not understand that I was taught by a witch from Kent, England; the Kent witches are pre-Gardenarian, and I didn't even know that until Stewart and Janet Farrar came to stay with us. They stayed with my daughters and I for almost four weeks one time, let them stay without doing anything because they had been on tour and they'd been treated kind of badly in America. Some groups that they went to see would have them sleeping in the back end of a restaurant; they weren't treated well. So I gave them my bedroom. I got up and made bacon and eggs every morning for him and her. I let them just rest here, you know, so they could just walk around and enjoy Salem. When I had long talks with Stewart, I started telling him about Felicity and how she taught me. Of course, it's changed a lot from what I learned; I mean that was very basic and you didn't call quarters. You didn't do any of that, it was all new. But we've added it in too. But I brought the science to witchcraft so we had this long talk; he says,

"Do you realize the witches of Kent are pre-Gardenarian, that your tradition is the oldest tradition in the world today?" I was totally flabbergasted because it didn't even dawn on me because I'm not in touch; there aren't any witches in Kent anymore and if they are, they're kind of modern; who knows what they are? Felicity's family can't be found; we've done all kinds of searches and there are people still searching, there are people going over there trying to find her family because she was my teacher. She lived in Boston, she was a librarian.

As I sat there, listening to Laurie speak about her past, it struck a chord in me.

Painting a Picture of Salem

I knew when Laurie first moved to Salem she had suffered some great injustices due to her beliefs and outspoken personality. So I wanted to make sure that was part of the interview. It seemed almost as if Laurie already had an understanding of what I wanted or needed to cover as she went straight into a story that painted a picture of the city as it looked when she first arrived.

This city was, believe me, it was in the Dark Ages when I moved here. Where you are sitting now (at Laurie's Wharf Street Shop, The Cat, The Crow, and The Crown) was a tank farm and all of the trucks going in and out filling the oil in their trucks. There was oil on the streets, it was a mess. It was ugly, all the houses around here, they hadn't been painted, the cellar windows were broken out, and cats and dogs going in and out. People had old mattresses on their porches. Except for Chestnut Street where they have the cute little fifties houses, but that's not even in town, that's not where people can see it. Everything around here was dilapidated and ugly and old.

The city itself, they always want to promote the maritime history because they don't understand that this is the only city in America where first it had a dark history, now it has a wonderful history of witches forming now.

I didn't mean to come here; I had divorced for the second time, I had two little girls, I denied my husband, and went on welfare so I didn't have to deal with him. I didn't have a job, I didn't have any way of earning a living, and I had to cope. I moved into the north end of Boston because I figured if I'm there, we can get to the museum and all sorts of things, and the market there for the food is cheaper and we could survive better. Welfare I had never heard of it really, I mean I had heard of it, but somebody suggested it to me; they said,

"Well why don't you do that, and that way you can cope for a while and then you can do something else." And that is exactly what I did. Well, while I was in the north end of Boston I had seen a shop on Cambridge Street in Boston at the base of Beacon Hill and I wanted to open my witch shop there but I couldn't—I didn't have any money, I had nothing. My second husband had squandered and lost my family money so I had nothing.

I'll Move Anywhere Except Salem

So I met this woman who had two children, a boy and a girl. She had divorced an engineer from Connecticut; she got $600 a month, which was a lot in those days for alimony, and she had moved to the north end. We met and she was so excited that I was a witch; she was very metaphysical herself, a nice person, so we got to be very, very good friends. She said, "You know what we should do? City isn't good for us and our kids. Why don't we rent a house in suburbia and share it, then our kids will have a yard and a better surrounding?" I said, "It's a great idea, I'll move anywhere except Salem, Massachusetts. I don't want to move there."

She said, "Okay, I understand." Well, two days later she comes with a newspaper rolled up and a circle around something. She said, "Promise me you'll look at this house." I said, "Of course." Never thinking she meant Salem. It was on Chestnut Street, the world's most architecturally perfect street is Chestnut Street and the first house that was ever built on Chestnut Street was up for rent, the whole house!

She said, "Just promise me." I said, "Okay, I'll look, I can't believe you did that." So we came to Salem and my daughter, Jody, had seen the house psychically before we came here, and described the whole thing. I walked in and I thought, *Oh who's gonna know, oh fine, I'll move here.*

Even though it was late '60s, I wore long black gowns. I didn't wear robes like I do now. I used to go to Filene's Basement and buy black evening gowns, usually ones with long sleeves, usually taffeta or something nothing with sequins, very plain. I had the first pentacle made, witches didn't wear pentacles, I had a jeweler make my pentacle, and witches never wore those—it's an Egyptian symbol. When my daughters were going to school, I used to use a magic marker and draw a pentacle on their undershirts to keep them protected.

I'll never forget after we moved to Salem, I had on a pair of black slacks and a black turtle neck sweater and I had this Austrian army coat; it was cool. It was fitted and came down long to your calf. I was skipping up the stairs to the post office and this man in a suit came out of the post office and he started to go down the stairs. He stopped and he looked at me and he looked at my pentacle and he looked back at me. I knew and he knew; he knew I was a witch and I don't know how he knew, but it was one of those moments, and he looked at me and it was like a revelation on his face. It was the first encounter I had anybody who was a stranger who looked at me and knew.

It is obvious to me what the witchcraft boom in Salem has done for the city—what Laurie started back in the 1960s and 70s has become a craze. Everywhere you turn when walking in downtown Salem there are witchcraft shops and Tarot readers, at least three on each street. Those decrepit houses and the seedy pictures that Laurie gives us of Salem's past are literally that, in the past. Now you walk down the street and see beautiful colonial homes with wonderfully manicured yards. All of this because of Laurie Cabot and the notoriety she brought to Salem? Yes, yes it is.

The Drunken Man and Her First Opportunity to Teach

Then I decided after we moved here that I was going to teach witchcraft as a science. I did a spell, a circle for that, I said, "My life's goal is to teach witchcraft as a science to the world." That's it. Right after that a girlfriend of mine who had her own band was singing in Rhode Island and she says, "You gotta come and listen to me sing and see the band." Well I kinda didn't want to go but I went. Here I am, sitting in this nightclub at their table and they are doing a set and I'm thinking to myself, "I'm so far away from home...what am I doing here?" Well at the next table is a guy who's totally drunk, he's slobbering his words. He kept looking over at me, and I kept looking away. He finally got up and came over and sat next to me, and for some reason I was polite to him and he said, "You're a witch aren't you?"' I said, "Yes, I am." And we started talking, I talked about my teaching unit and how I wanted to teach. He says, "Well, I'm head of Continuing Ed at Wellesley High School. Why don't you send me a curriculum?"

I thought, *This is why I'm in Rhode Island*, and then I thought, *Yeah, right*. He wrote down his address and phone number and everything and I thought, *Sure, mister*. When I went home, I looked at that name and address and I thought, *Maybe it's an answer to my spell*. So I put together the first teaching unit of teaching alpha, *Witchcraft I, II, and III*. I had a friend of mine type it up; it looked very neat, very professional; I sent it to him. I taught for ten weeks in Wellesley High School and I had the cream of Wellesley society women and men coming to my class because they had heard about it and that was my first teaching job.

A small look into the life of Laurie Cabot. *Picture courtesy of Laurie Cabot.*

Molly-Boo Pushes Laurie Out of the Broom Closet

We were living on Chestnut Street across from the mayor, but nobody knew. So one day, I had Molly-boo and Sabrina—they were both black kitties—and molly-boo goes up the tree. You can still see the tree next to the house; it's four stories high she went; she couldn't come down. It rained, it thundered, it lightening, it hailed! It did everything! And she couldn't come down. Sabrina, the other black cat would climb up the tree lick her (Molly-boo), go halfway down backwards, and turn around and jump down, but she still wouldn't come down. I was so upset, and so afraid for her, of course. After three days and nights, she's gonna be weak. Pretty soon she's gonna fall out of the tree or die. I called the fire department. "We have a union. You'll never see a cat skeleton in a tree. We don't do that anymore." I called the police—they said the exact same thing. I called the Animal Rescue League here and there was a man and he said, "I'm seventy years old. I haven't been on the truck for twenty years. I don't go out and rescue cats."

Now I'm like so panicked, you can imagine how I felt—no one's gonna help me. On the third floor of our house I'd open the bathroom window, I put a plank across; of course she wasn't gonna walk across the plank. But I tried; I tried to call her to get down. I'm saying, "Hunny, you've got to come down." I'm yelling out the window. I'm standing at the bottom of the tree. Sabrina's going up and down trying to get Molly-boo to follow her. Now I've had it, I thought, *These son of a bitches, how can they do this? How can they not have the compassion?*

I called up the *Salem Evening News*; I would never have done this, but I called the paper because I wanted to save her life and this guy answered. His name was Dan; he never answers the phone; he was a photographer. He answered the phone and I said, "My name is Laurie Cabot, and I live at 18 Chestnut Street and my cat is in a tree four stories up, and I'm very upset. I called the fire department..." I told him the whole story. And I said, "And I'm a witch," the very last of it, it came out of my mouth. I said, "I'm a witch and that's my familiar, and I want her down now!"

He said, "Hello? Excuse me? Can I call you right back?" and I said, "Okay." Then I went, Oh my god! But I knew I had to do something. It didn't dawn on me what that would do. Next thing I know I hear noise outside. I look out the window, there's the fire department, the police, the little old man in the truck, and the photographer—and they were all looking up at Molly-boo. I walked outside and they said, "Don't put a curse on me." I said, "Look that's not what I do, and besides all I care about is that cat up there."

So the little old man gets a cat pole with a loop on it and says, "Take me upstairs where you've got that plank." I brought him to the third floor in the bathroom, open the window, he sticks the cat pole out puts the noose over her head brings her in and puts her in my arms. Two seconds, Molly-boo is in my arms, after all that. Well the next day in the paper, 'cause he did take a picture of us in the house, on the back page is a picture of us. It went *United Press International*, every associated press; everyone around the globe got that picture. Molly-boo outed me, that was the beginning."

Opening Up Shop

Laurie did a lot of firsts for witches, some that even I wasn't aware of. I don't know that she was aware the entire time that she was making strides for those in alternative religions. Nonetheless she did. I asked her about the first witch shop she opened, its original location on Derby Street in Salem, Massachusetts. The shop only lasted about a year, but its impact was felt all around the world.

What happened was that when I came here there were no witch shops in America—I opened the first one. And I didn't come here to do that; I moved here thinking that no one would know I was a witch. But I made a vow to the Goddess to wear all black, to wear my robes and my pentacle. So when I opened the shop, I didn't even realize, I was very naïve, that it was natural, it was Salem and a witch. So the media came here next thing; I know it's *UPI*, *Associated Press*, worldwide people from other countries, all kinds of journalists came from France, England, and Australia, you can't even imagine.

I have to be honest; I walked away from this interview feeling empowered, intrigued, and rather blessed to be able to sit and listen to the stories of Laurie's life, both personal and public. I wanted to find out about the second teaching gig she got at Salem State College and what an opportunity like that meant to her.

Then I meet up with a young girl from St. Ceridian's, one of the Catholic schools. She brought a couple of girlfriends to the shop when I opened the store; they wanted to take a classes and I said "Fine;" so I started teaching classes with them. Then one day she says, "My mother and father want to meet you." I said, "They do? Fine, someday I would like that—someday."

She says, "Come with me."

I said, "Oh, okay." He was the dean of Salem State College and I didn't know that.

She says, "Oh yeah, my dad calls it LCU, Laurie Cabot University, when I come to do classes with you."

I go and I meet with him; the next thing I know he says, "I want a sixteen-week curriculum you're going to teach at Continuing Ed and the next year you will have an accredited course at Salem State College."

Well, I got to do the sixteen weeks, but the board of trustees, because of the publicity, the pictures of me standing at the board teaching in the state college in my robes and everything—well it went around the globe—and the board of trustees said, "No, no, no, no, there's too much publicity." So I wasn't allowed to have my accredited course. But it taught the world, because it made the world news. So witchcraft as a science was out there."

A Stand For Justice

I wanted to know what exactly caused Laurie to raise her voice and proclaim that witches deserved to be protected. So I did what any normal human being would do, I asked. Laurie never talks like she is a victim, but some of the things she told me about made me cringe a little. Much like the witches in 1692, the town of Salem was willing to repeat its history, maybe not to the extreme, but the essence of "witch-hate" was still rife.

When I moved to Salem and I opened the store, I'd be walking down the street with my two little girls, and people would lean out the window and say, "they oughta hang you again" in front of my daughters. One time it was Thanksgiving and I was getting turkey stuff in the supermarket and this man starts screaming at me, "You don't belong in here you devil worshiper" and I stayed quiet because my daughters were with me. We went through the checkout and everybody was just quiet. The girl behind the counters didn't know what to do, nobody knew what to do. They were scared and they were embarrassed for him and for me, I think, and they didn't know whether they should be throwing me out. So after all of that I realized that nobody knows what a witch is or who they are; they have all of these Christian ideas and they're so inundated with it, they are so fanatic about it, that it's got to be explained. And we have a civil right; we're not in 1692, you're not going to hang us, you're not going to harass me in the supermarket because you're not harassing the Catholic standing next to me. It's not going to happen; I know about the constitution. So that's what did it, every witch has a right be protected under the law. If someone harasses me, I have the right to call 911: "Someone is harassing me—make them stop or take them away." Well at that point the police didn't know that it was a real religion or that they had to protect us. They had no idea there were cities and towns where the authorities had no idea, still.

Laurie continued to talk about not just her experiences, but the experiences of those witches she helped within her community. She said that Project Witches Protection which is run now by Richard Corvino, Rev. Mark Stab, and Rev. Rhonda Flynn who all maintain a status of either High Priest or Priestess, continue to educate and help those who are being afflicted by prejudices concerning their religious practices. The group sends out over 300 pamphlets a month to law enforcement, state, school, and city officials to help educate leaders in understanding the law concerning witchcraft.

> We ask witches in other states and areas if they are having a problem in their area, or before they have a problem, to give us the names and addresses of all the authorities in their cities so we can provide materials to them so that they will know the law. The local newspaper, *FYI*, let's send them a packet so they know what the law is, that has made such a difference—it made a difference in this town because we had a couple of incidences. A young witch moved into town, and he had a couple of roommates who weren't so great and the police came looking for one of the roommates. Well his athame was on the mantel piece with his chalice and they took his athame because you can't have a four-inch double-sided blade in Massachusetts. You can't carry it, or have it; it's illegal. He came to see me; he was crying cause he had had it for years; it was something his mother gave him or something. I marched down to the police station; I gave them the law memorandum. I said, "That is a religious item," and they gave it back to him. And they started understanding how to protect the witches in Salem. So they do, like when we do the candle light walk from Gallows Hill. It was an outdoor circle where anybody can come for Samhain, and then we march back into town with candles down to the cemetery and we put a wreath where we honor the people who died. Which is okay; they died for our freedom too, even if they may not have been witches, they died because of us, so we honor them. Now we have a police escort and the police drive and they walk with us, so nobody can harass us.

Legal intern Patricia Barki wrote the pamphlet or FYI; it outlines the laws and case files that made those rules which protect witchcraft as a religion. In an interview with Joe O'Connell from the *Salem News*, Rev. Rhonda Flynn, Treasurer for the *PWP*, says, "People have lost custody of their children because of the fact that they practice." The PWP looks to defend and aid all witches who feel their rights have been taken away.

Laurie knows she can't reach everyone though, as much as she may try. Personally, I am thoroughly heartened by the work they do. Completely on a donation basis, Cabot says in the same interview, "Quite a few people have donated, but it doesn't defray the cost of mailing. It is one thing to be afforded civil rights; it is another thing to claim them." Rick Corvino says, "It is one of the most abused and exploited religions." Part of the reason? We let it happen. Laurie is right in this, if you feel that you are being held down or repressed because of your religious beliefs, contact the PWP—the info is in the back of this book. Think of it like a Witches Union; they have your back.

The Witches Protection League

Prior to Project Witch Protection, Laurie had another anti-discrimination group called The Witches League of Public Awareness. I had to know how Laurie Cabot felt when she conducted her first protest with the WLPA, after finding it splashed all over newspapers and on television in response to *The Witches of Eastwick*, the movie that starred Cher, Michelle Pfeiffer, and Susan Sarandon, based on the novel of the same name by John Upton, which was being filmed right in Laurie's backyard. The protest was held at the Massachusetts state film bureau.

Astonished, amazed, happy. It felt...it's like it was all worth it. Even though I exposed my daughters to a mother wearing a cape and a robe standing out in the public and they saw all the ridicule, it was vindication really for them that the witches came forward and said "we protest, we're standing up."

There was a sense of humility as Laurie spoke, like this was something that had to be done.

It was wonderful. I just feel that anyone can change the world; anyone, if you have the courage to open your mouth and state your claim. You can change things; you really can, and then another voice joins yours. If you're silent, it's never going to happen. Anyone can do it if they have the courage to follow up on their convictions. They have to; it's not just me. Anyone can do it. I was thrilled to find that out, I was thrilled to know that I could make a difference. It is what I wanted to do. It's my job; it's my goal in life to make a difference for all witches everywhere in the world. To have them recognized for all the good that they do, recognized for their ability to heal, that we don't do any harm.

The Official Witch of Salem Meets the Queen of Talk

With all of the press Laurie and The Witches League of Public Awareness garnered during their protests, immediately, Cabot was launched into the rounds of daytime television talk shows—one of which was a very memorable episode of *The Oprah Winfrey Show* which aired on June 24, 1987. The title of the episode was simply "Witches." Laurie was in the position of going head to head with Bob Larsen, a Christian Minister and Joseph Marquis; a former Satanic High Priest turned born-again Christian. Finishing the panel was Whitley Strieber (author and UFO abductee) and Dora Ruffner a white witch.

Oprah's talk show that day started out with a focus on the movie, *The Witches of Eastwick*, and ended in heated debate between Laurie and Bob. Oprah turned from interviewer to referee within ten or fifteen minutes into the show. She began by defending *The Witches of Eastwick*, saying that actor Jack Nicholson perceived the project to be light-hearted, and he did not believe that it left the audience thinking witches were bad. Laurie on the other hand had to disagree, believing that by showing these "witches" doing negative things with their abilities only furthered the myth that witches were evil. Laurie equated it to, Native Americans in the western movies who were always seen as the bad people or not good enough to be the heroes. She also went on to talk about the kids' program, *My Little Pony*, that had just been released at that time. In the story lines there were, "three bad witches, not three bad Buddhists and not three bad Baptists, you know."

Laurie also defended the position of witches wearing black robes, equating it with nuns, rabbis and priests who also don black clothing.

Joseph Marquis said that from the age of five he had been a practicing witch. It began with someone sending a demon to him. Though he skips the bulk of the story behind the demon, he does talk about how initially he went at witchcraft as an earth-based religion similar to what many witches practice. However, he insisted that once someone started to reach the higher levels of magic, that the philosophy and ideas began to change. He proclaimed that upon ascending to these levels a person would then learn who was really worshiped – the devil, Lucifer, or Satan – and that he believed that the Illuminati have some strange connection to witchcraft. This surprised the heck out of me, as most Illuminati members from my research and understanding were scientists, philosophers, and devout atheists.

[Actually, there were established connections at one point between Masons and Illuminati (supposedly) and many of the Masons felt conflicted because of the atheistic Illuminati. So...one might ask, did they really worship a Devil or God they did not believe in? I hate to add this point in but I feel it is very important, as he is associating Illuminati with witchcraft and I really feel the need to put in my two cents. He implied that Charles Manson killing Sharon Tate was an Illuminati hit and that Manson is one of the greatest wizards that has ever lived. Personally, I could not believe that he even thought to bring Manson or those despicable murders into the conversation at all. Since he did, I figured I would address it. One piece of evidence he believed supported this fact was how Sharon Tate was found – which was in a position he believed to carry an eerie similarity to the Hanged Man in the standard Tarot deck. While Marquis infers that Sharon was hung in the position, of the Hanged Man, I must disagree. Both she and Sebring were hung by the neck, not the feet. Sharon was stabbed repeatedly in the chest and back. He also asserted that four of the high holidays within the witchcraft religious structure were meant for human sacrifice and detailed how to pick someone up, drug him or her, and kill them. It really upset me to read some of the portions of this transcript. It is not that I disbelieve his story; I am sure to him it is very real. It takes a lot to get up on Oprah's stage, or any stage for that matter, and speak about your beliefs. However, I do not agree with many of the things he had to say and neither did Laurie or Whitley Streiber.]

Many of you are probably wondering how an alien abductee like Whitley Streiber ended up on the Oprah set defending witchcraft. While writing *Cat Magic*, he got in touch with Margot Adler who introduced him to many within the craft. Initially, he came at witches with the same ideas as most of the mainstream population. Ready to paint the picture of a snaggle-toothed, green-faced villain, Whitley's mind was soon changed after meeting some of the actual practitioners. He stated that when you strip away all of the fears, superstitions, and the negative imagery, witchcraft at its essence was simply another human religion.

Laurie, Whitley, and Dora really did a wonderful job establishing witchcraft's position as a positive spiritual belief system. However, Bob Larsen, a Christian Minister, came full force with the words of his God – time and again trying to attack witchcraft. When asked some very pointed questions, he went straight to Bible verses. No real answers were given.

In the end, Laurie got her say; she also one-upped the rest of the panel making appearances on Oprah three times altogether and even says she predicted the queen of talk's rise to fame (pre-syndication) in an interview with James Horrigan from the Boston Globe back in 2004.

I will let you form your own opinion of how the talk show went for Laurie and you can read more about Joseph and Bob's statements. I am putting here for your pleasure the website where I found the transcript. Enjoy! http://www.skepticfiles.org/mys4/oprah.htm.

Into The Night

Laurie Cabot is getting older now, with two grown daughters. She sits in her Wharf Street shop *The Cat, The Crow and The Crown,* and looking over her papers, helping patrons and answering questions in her soft almost hypnotic voice, but she is slowly fading into the mist as one of our last connections to the historic times of the pagan movement. I personally feel that a lot of people have begun to forget Laurie Cabot, forget what she has done for witches all over the world, heck even right in her own town.

I believe that Laurie Cabot is a Grand Dame of her faith, a healer on all levels, who has fought for justices big and small for her community. I am not surprised she feels an affinity with Queen Boudicca, who also had two daughters and stood up for her people by taking on the whole of the Roman army.

Who made it safe for them to stand up for themselves? Myself and my two daughters. I feel like Queen Boudicca; you know she was the last warrior queen of England and she had two warrior daughters fighting next to her. She was defeated, but she nearly won a war over the Romans. She was fabulous; she stood up for the rights of everybody in England. I always hope we win rather than lose, but I kind of think about that because I have my two daughters beside me and we all three stood up. My daughters learned to stand up for their rights; they learned to promote who they are in a good way.

Laurie talked about her feelings around some of the more outspoken and opinionated people in her community and their views of her:

I don't care what they say; you know they call me the "glitter witch" because we use glitter for magick, and then, "Oh, she is too theatrical; she wears to much makeup." Well, it's my choice; it's not about witchcraft especially. However, the magickal people out of Egypt wore the eye makeup because it was part of the God and the Goddess, and Scota was the first chieftain's wife of Scotland; Scotland is named after a Pharoah's daughter. They're digging up some of her artifacts now in Scotland. I have two friends; I don't see them that often. They are an old man and woman—they are genetists. They're like two Einsteins, they're so funny and they travel the world. Every once in a while they will come into the store, every two or three years. One day, I was sitting here and I didn't know about the DNA; I understood that Scota was the first chieftain's wife of Scotland and I was

Boadicea Haranguing the Britons by John Opie.

Laurie Cabot with author, Katie Boyd.

thinking about it. They walked in here and I had my door open, and they peeked their heads in here and they said, "If you're Scot, your DNA is Egyptian you know," and kept going. The chills went right up my spine; they'd answered what was brewing in my head about it, but I didn't even realize that. No wonder I had an affinity to things magickally Egyptian. I'm part Egyptian, I'm part Scot.

This fiery American-Scottish-Egyptian witch with a love of cats and a soft voice has certainly raised the bar for the next generation of witchcraft activists. She held the first witch's funeral in Murphy's Funeral Home in Salem, the first Witches Ball, wore the first pentacle, opened the first witch shop, set up the first anti-defamation league, held the first magick circle in public, she was the first to teach in a state college. With everything, Laurie has accomplished, she is happy to have seen these things happen and she still does not take credit for it.

These things just happened; you know what I mean. It's like the Gods and Goddesses pushed me into these things. That's how I got here.

Our Fathers of the Craft

There have been witches in all ages and countries. That is, there have been men and women who have had a knowledge of cures, philtres, charms and love potions and at times poisons. Sometimes it was believed they could affect the weather, bringing rain or drought. At times they were hated, at times they were loved; at times they were highly honoured, at times persecuted. They claimed to be, or were credited with being, in communication with the world of spirits, the dead, and sometimes with the lesser gods.

~ Gerald B. Gardner
"Witchcraft Today," 1954

Just like our mother's of the old religion, there were also some men who introduced another side of the Craft and helped to push the belief system further. These men brought the old teaching back into the mainstream and showed us many different branches of the Old Religion. Each of these men changed the outlook of the craft and made a difference in the freedom and path of witches today.

Gerald Gardner

Father of Modern Wicca

Established One of the First Recognized

Witchcraft Traditions

What matters most to me about Gerald Gardner isn't his *Book of Shadows* or where he took the information from; and honestly, there are so many different sources and opinions that are claiming to be facts. Yes, there is historical evidence which shows to us that some of Gardner's work was definitely not his own, that he may or may not have had close ties with Aleister Crowley, and that he published *Ye Book of Magickal Art* as a fiction book called *High Magic's Aid.*

The man whose hair resembled genius Albert Einstein's was a genius himself. Some theorize that delving into the Art was seen as a relaxing post-retirement hobby after working in rubber plantations. Gardner himself says that his rituals and learning was passed to him from a woman named Dorothy Clutterbuck. Doreen Valiente later confirmed this after Gardner died by finding the actual birth certificate, but whether it was *the* Dorothy will never be known. Before World War II, the word "witch" was not uttered, occult surely, Hermetic definitely, but witch…never. Those practitioners of the Old Religion still hid from the mainstream, conducting their rituals and spells, never uttering a word and keeping a strict code of silence. Understandably, as the Witchcraft Act of 1735 was still in effect, effectively, allowing for the continued persecution of witches.

A Brief Biography of the Man

Gerald Brousseau Gardner was born on June 13th, 1884 to a middle class family, with four brothers (only three of which lived at home)—you can imagine the chaos that erupted on a daily basis. Gardner's father ran Joseph Gardner and Sons, the oldest and most respected importer of hardwoods in the country. They had with them an Irish nursemaid who helped to look after the children. Gardner suffered from asthma in his early life; this Irish nurse lovingly nicknamed "Com," offered to take Gerald to warmer climates hoping to improve the poor boy's health. Gerald's parents agreed, and so in 1891, Gardner and his nursemaid took a trip to the Canary Islands, then Ghana, and finally Portugal. During this time, "Com" whose real name was Josephine, kept one eye on Gerald and the other out for an unwed man to marry. Eventually, she did marry; his name was David Elkington from Sri Lanka (then known as Ceylon) in 1900.

The Gardners agreed that Gerald could go and live with his nursemaid in the warmer climates on a more permanent basis. With Com's marriage came the tea plantation called Ladbroke Estate.

Gerald thrived there for a time. Five years later, at the age of 21, he was shipped back to Britain and he became acquainted with the Surgensons a branch of the family that Gerald had been told to stay away from. His parents didn't like them because they were Methodists, but Gerald found their philosophies, theories, and ready discussion of the paranormal fascinating.

It's in the Blood

It was from this side of the family that Gardner first heard the word *witch* in any type of relation to him. Ted Surgenson, the patriarch of the family, mentioned at one point that whispers among the family had led to the belief that Gerald's grandfather, Joseph, was a witch. Also, that an ancestor of theirs, Grissell Gairdner, had been burned as a witch in Newburgh in 1610.

Gerald headed back to Sri Lanka and stayed there until near the end of 1908. He then got restless and decided to travel some more. Still, the word *witch* burned in the back of his mind. The thought that he could have ancestors, not to mention his grandfather, who were witches astounded him.

Borneo greatly influenced Gardner and fed his growing interest in anthropology; there he met a tribe of headhunters called the Dyaks. Gerald grew close with them and was intrigued by their way of life, specifically their rituals, spiritual beliefs, and rites of passage.

Around The World

Travel was one of the great loves of Gerald Gardner. A Gemini, by nature he was a curious man and in 1911, he set off for a holiday trip to Malaya. He ended up being offered a job there and decided to settle down for a little while. Between 1911 and 1927, Gardner was introduced to a man named Cornwall, who had converted to Islam and had become a local of Malaya, marrying a Malayan woman. In 1916, Gerald returned to Britain once again to try and help in World War I. Originally, he tried to join the Royal Navy, but due to his health issues he could not, so he decided to work at a hospital which treated injured soldiers. While there, he caught malaria and his efforts were immediately stopped. He then returned back home to Malaya, and gave his job as a rubber planter up and became instead an inspector of rubber farms for the government. He was shot at a few times for his efforts.

In 1920, Gerald's mother died, although he did not return home for that occasion. He did in 1927 when he found out his father was ill. There Gardner redeveloped his affinity for all things spiritual. He decided to attend a Spiritualist Church and began to get more involved in mediumship and spiritualism as a whole. He did claim to have a few encounters with relatives who were deceased whilst at the same time decrying the bulk of what he experienced at the church, although he did admit to a few genuine experiences. The same year he met and married Dorothea Rosedale also known as Donna. They honeymooned on the Isle of Wight before leaving for France and then onto Malaya.

Already Gardner had a belief in the otherworldly but the ritual of the local Malayans really instilled a belief of magick. Gardner quickly made a name for himself as he began studying the early civilizations of the Malaya and their ritual tools. His real passion lay in the keris which he ended up writing papers about and finally a book in 1936 entitled *Keris and Other Malay Weapons*. In it he discusses the origin of this weapon among others and the process behind making the blades, sheaths, and hilts. He also speaks about a symbol found on the keris which is to represent an elephant god and how he believed that many of the Malaya still used it as a symbol of luck. But the cool stuff is at the back of the book where he talks about invulnerability and the talismans and beliefs held by the Malay people to accomplish this feat:

Invulnerability is conferred:

(1) By use of certain objects

(a) kĕlambu rasul Allah (the prophets bed curtain) a sleeveless fighting jacket embroidered with pious texts

(b) kĕris bērtuwah: these especially k. majapahit and k. pichit conferred on their owners pĕrambut sēnjata or invulnerability to weapons

Gardner goes on to speak about a magical piece of weaponry (which he seemed to have in his possession at the time) and how it is the crème de la crème of conferred invulnerability.

bĕsi kuning (little yellow iron) a legendary metal, probably bronze. It is always said to be harder than iron and a good bonze weapon would probably be harder than a primitive iron one. I possess an ancient bronze blade that is said to be bĕsi kuning but this claim is not admitted by most Malays who have seen it, as they very sensibly say:

We have never seen bĕsi kuning, only heard of it and don't know what it looks like. The only way to test it is to wear it and get someone to shoot at you, at close range, and if it prevents your being hurt it is bĕsi kuning. I have not made this test yet.

He also said that its invulnerability will be bestowed on a child who is born with a complete caul (born in its amniotic sac). Also he talks about the incantations that aid in gaining invulnerability. His interests in archaeology and the ancient belief systems were brought back with him to England when he retired in 1936. He and Donna moved to the New Forest area.

A Biography of The Witch

Gardner claimed to have been initiated into witchcraft in 1939 during that same year he also joined the Folklore Society. His first write up for their newsletter was printed in July of 1939 and was regarding witchcraft relics. While traveling around Churchill, Gardner came upon the Rosicrucian Order Crotona Fellowship; he joined their theater and states that this is where he met members of the New Forest Coven that he ended up being initiated into. Also in 1939, he wrote his first fiction book, *A Goddess Arrives*, followed in 1949 by *High Magics Aid*. Disguised as another fiction book, Gardner incorporates the magic of King Solomon and other occult figures as well as some of his own.

Introduction of High Magic's Aid

"Magic! Witchcraft! Stuff and nonsense. No one believes in such things nowadays. It was all burning evil-smelling powders, muttering words. The Devil jumped up, and you sold him your soul. That was all there was to it." But was that really all? Would any sane person— or insane, for that matter—sell their souls to eternal fire for nothing or nearly nothing?

Latimers in Highcliffe, where Gardner was supposedly initiated into the Craft.

Our forefathers had faith. At least about nine million of them suffered a cruel death, mainly by being burnt alive, because of this belief.

Magic is sometimes defined as attempting to do something contrary to the laws of nature, to bring success to various undertakings.

Now the Church taught this could be done by prayers and offerings to the saints. It was also an article of faith that King Solomon evoked great spirits and forced them to perform many wonders. Books were also written on similar subjects.

The Key of Solomon the King, the most widely used book of magic, was believed to be written by King Solomon himself. Perhaps the next most widely used was the *Enchiridion* of Pope Leo III.

If the great ones of the earth practised it and taught you to do likewise, should not the lesser ones also believe it could be done safely, if they only knew the way?

Art magic was taught more or less publicly at various universities, and, secretly, almost everywhere.

You might ask: "But did it work? If not, why did they believe it?"

But they saw innumerable cases where magical ritual seemed to work. When France was prostrate at the feet of England, her king had no men, money, hope, or followers. A young peasant girl, the Witch of Domremy, apparently drew armies from the ground, and drove out the invaders; that she was burnt alive as a witch for so doing, only strengthened the belief that it worked, if one only knew how and dared risk it.

Pope Innocent III was made Pope some time before he was even a priest. Stephen Langton, an utterly unknown man, suddenly became Archbishop of Canterbury overnight. This smelled of magic to our forefathers.

Would you know what they believed and attempted to achieve? Then come with me into the past.

~Gerald B. Gardner

In 1951, the Witchcraft Act had been repealed and followers of the ancient traditions began to slowly come out of hiding. Although the Witchcraft Act was no longer a threat, the people of the United Kingdom still held onto their negative beliefs regarding witchcraft. Gardner, having copied the *Book of Shadows* from the New Forest coven, struck out on his own. The book was fragmented and he filled it in with those resources he was familiar with such as Aleister Crowley, of which he was a member of the OTO. One cannot fault him for looking for answers in other parts of the occult as what he had to work with was incomplete, but he then went on to claim it as his own. Doreen Valiente later disproved and helped him revise expunging Crowley's influence in the book.

In 1952, he and his wife moved to the Isle of Man at the behest of Cecil Williamson who offered Gardner the position of Director and Resident Witch of his museum filled with relics of witchcraft. Gardner was honored at first but soon felt that Williamson was trying to capitalize on the hype around witches.

In 1954, Gardner bought the museum from Williamson, who then went on to open another museum on the mainland. Gardner restocked this museum with artifacts from his own private collection. After the success of *High Magic's Aid*, Gardner decided to write a straightforward witch instructional in 1954 called *Witchcraft Today*. Then in 1959, he wrote *The Meaning of Witchcraft*. In this book he describes how he met and was initiated into the Old Religion and the reasons why they initially did not want him to talk about his involvement (or theirs) in the Craft.

However, after Dr. Murray's books appeared, some other people were bold enough to admit that there were some witches left, but said that they were only village fortune-tellers, imposters who knew nothing about the subject, and there never had been any organization, and anyone who thought otherwise was just being imaginative.

I was of these opinions in 1939, when, here in Britain, I met some people who compelled me to alter them. They were interested in curious things, reincarnation for one, and they were also interested in the fact that an ancestress of mine, Grizel Gairdner, had been burned as a witch. They kept saying that they had met me before. We went through everywhere we had been, and I could not ever have met them before in this life; but they claimed to have known me in previous lives. Although I believe in reincarnation, as many people do who have lived in the East, I do not remember my past lives clearly; I only wish I did. However, these people told me enough to make me think. Then some of these new (or old) friends said, "You belonged to us in the past. You are of the blood. Come back to where you belong."

I realised that I had stumbled on something interesting; but I was half-initiated before the word "Wica" which they used hit me like a thunderbolt, and I knew where I was, and that the Old Religion still existed. And so I found myself in the Circle, and there took the usual oath of secrecy, which bound me not to reveal certain things.

In this way I made the discovery that the witch cult, that people thought to have been persecuted out of existence, still lived. I found, too, what it was that made so many of our ancestors dare imprison-

The sculpture of the Wiccan Horned God at the Museum of Witchcraft. *Picture courtesy of Midnightblueowl.*

The Witches Mill then and now. Modern Image taken in 2008 – many thanks to Tof, author of *Gerald Gardner et le Culte des Sorcières*

The Witches Mill then and now. Modern Image taken in 2008 – many thanks to Tof, author of *Gerald Gardner et le Culte des Sorcières*.

ment, torture, and death rather than give up the worship of the Old Gods and the love of the old ways. I discovered the inner meaning of that saying in one of Fiona MacLeod's books: "The Old Gods are not dead. They think we are."

I am a member of the Society for Psychical Research, and on the Committee of the Folklore Society; so I wanted to tell of my discovery. But I was met with a determined refusal. "The Age of Persecution is not over," they told me; "give anyone half a chance and the fires will blaze up again." When I said to one of them, "Why do you keep all these things so secret still? There's no persecution nowadays!" I was told, "Oh, isn't there? If people knew what I was, every time a child in the village was ill, or somebody's chickens died, I should get the blame for it. Witchcraft doesn't pay for broken windows."

And to explain exactly what prompted him to write the book *Witchcraft Today*:

> In 1952, Pennethorne Hughes wrote a book, *Witchcraft*, which gave a very good historical account of witchcraft, but stated that while in mediaeval times witches had a fully worked-out rituals of their own which they performed, modern witches were simply perverts who celebrated "Black Masses," which he described as being blasphemous imitations of the Christian Mass. This made some of my friends very angry, and I managed to persuade them that it might do good to write a factual book about witchcraft, and so I wrote *Witchcraft Today*. In writing this latter book, I soon found myself between Scylla and Charybdis. If I said too much, I ran the risk of offending people whom I had come to regard highly as friends. If I said too little, the publishers would not be interested. In this situation I did the best I could. In particular, I denied that witches celebrated the Black Mass, or that they killed animals—or even unbaptised babies—as blood sacrifices.

Gardner's belief system quickly spread. Today, the word "Wicca" is one spoken around the world, mentioned in movies, television shows, and more. Gardner became an accidental leader of thousands of witches during his generations and millions in the next. He laid down the foundation for all modern witches with his ideas of casting circles, ritual swords, and other elements. He introduced the skyclad forms of ritual, taking initiative from his love of naturism; he changed witchcraft completely with his books, interviews, odd and enchanting personality. Gardner passed away in 1964 whilst travelling home from Lebanon, the *News of the World* wrote an article about his death:

★ WOMAN'S VIEW ★

By JEAN MACAULAY

DAY I MET A WITCH...

THE witch lowered himself into a straight-backed chair with a chuckle.

"Wicca," he corrected. "Not witch—wicca."

I nodded. After all, it isn't every day I meet a witch. In fact, Dr. Gerald Gardner is the first witc . . . wicca . . . I have ever met.

And he looks the part. No one could be ordinary with a head like this Elder Wicca's.

Whenever light catches it the shock of white hair shines like a halo, shadowing the fine-featured face, the remarkable eyes and long, narrow white beard.

Light kept filtering through the window of the 400-year-old barn he uses as a study in Castletown, Isle of Man.

SINISTER SWORD

It picked on the silver candlesticks, the magic knife, the old books on magic, and the heavy, sinister-looking black sword.

Then I got a shock! This self-confessed, severely-criticised witch told me he is a Scot.

It is 72 years since he left the

But nothing's eerie about this spellbinder

parental home in North Berwick. The skeleton in the family cupboard was his grandfather in North Berwick, who was a witch.

The confidence made the room feel almost cosy, and the wicca willingly corrected the superstitious nonsense I have heard about witches and their craft.

WISE WICCAS

Witches — or wiccas — are "wise people" and are quite distinct from magicians. Magicians call up "non-human intelligence," but witches work under their own power.

And witches do NOT effect evil. They work in unison to cast spells to ensure a good harvest, to protect a friend in danger or to well-wish someone in trouble.

But the man himself interested me a lot more than the art 200 people in Scotland are practising NOW. Because he is a spellbinder.

Only his magic is the kind found in any eloquent traveller who has spent 77 years seeking the answers to a million questions, living in many

GERALD GARDNER at work in his 400-year-old study.

strange places and seeing many strange things.

STRANGE TALES

Many strange stories are told on the island—of this man, of the witches who gather and perform strange ceremonies, and of the punishment meted out to any witch who tries to use power to do harm.

But Gerald Gardner impresses me most as a scholar— probably because of his striking resemblance to the late George Bernard Shaw.

Only G.B.S. was never known to wear a magic ring or a heavy bronze bracelet which tells other witches that their colleague is an Elder Witch.

A 1961 article by a Scottish reporter Jean Macaulay entitled "The Day I Met a Witch." *Courtesy of Melissa Harrington and Melissa Seims.*

Dr. Gerald Brosseau Gardner points to exhibits in the witchcraft museum at Witches' Mill, Castletown.

YES,

CASTLETOWN.
Wednesday Night.

IN my time I've met quite a few witches. Gold diggers and double-crossers and heart-breakers. Now I have talked with a self-professed witch—a MAN, at that.

It was a strange experience. I shall never forget his angular face, nor his piercing blue eyes. Nor the setting of the interview.

Manxland is rich in folklore about fairies and " little people " in the glens and witches. But no 20th century human being has dared to admit: " I am a witch." No one, except GERALD BROSSEAU GARDNER. He says he is a Doctor of Philosophy, an honorary degree conferred on him by Singapore University 20 years ago.

The sun had gone down and it was a cold evening when I drove through the countryside, to halt at a four-roomed cottage in a narrow street here.

Wica

To the door came a six-footer. He looked like a benevolent grandee. He has a shock of white hair and a Van Dyck beard. He wore a green pullover, open-neck shirt, check trousers and brown shoes. I said: " Dr. Gardner, I presume? "

" Come in," he invited. His voice was gentle, his manner warm.

He sank back into an armchair and gripped its sides. I could not help noticing his deep-set, piercing eyes. On the third finger of each hand was a heavy ring; a bronze bracelet rested on his wrist. I asked whether he had any other adornments. He showed his tattooed arms—a snake, an anchor, a dragon and a dagger.

Here we were, in his kitchen. Big logs lay unburned in the fireplace. Daggers, spears, and other weapons hung on the walls.

Straight away I began: "Are

The *Daily Dispatch* August 5, 1954 newspaper. *Courtesy of Melissa Harrington and Melissa Seims.*

To other passengers aboard the steamer sailing slowly off the African coast he was just a strange old man appearing as usual in the breakfast lounge. A grey goatee beard, strange piercing eyes and a frail form. He was some "old writer" who had been wintering in Lebanon and the ship had picked him up at Beirut. When he collapsed and died over the breakfast table there was the usual flurry. Hurried consultations ended in the inevitable decision that he should be buried in the next port of call.

He was buried in Tunis last week – but not before distant relatives in Tennessee USA, had frantically cabled the Foreign Office about one Dr. Gerald Brosseau Gardner, aged 80, self-confessed witch, keeper of the museum of witchcraft at Castletown, Isle of Man and author of books on witchcraft.

Weekend magazine June 24-26, 1957. *Courtesy of Melissa Harrington and Melissa Seims.*

In Britain, upon hearing of Gardner's death, came a time of tumultuous meetings, grief, and anger as they all came to terms with the fact that their unofficial leader had passed on. In the same article, a Mrs. Eleanor Bone speaks of how the covens were at that time trying to organize a meeting to essentially elect the next leader. She said:

> Our intention now is to form a central committee for English witches and I shall probably be voted the liason officer between all covens.

Gardner to me was really a man who helped to kick start the witch phenomenon, opening people's minds and hearts to the idea of witchcraft as a true religion. He brought people to realize that when they speak of the Craft, they can speak in present terms, not just anthropologically, that there are witches NOW, that there will be in the FUTURE and that through all of the devastation, witchcraft has and will SURVIVE.

Britain's chief witch dies at sea

News of the World Reporter *February 23rd, 1964.*

TO the other passengers aboard the steamer sailing slowly off the North African coast he was just a strange old man appearing as usual in the breakfast lounge.

A grey goatee beard, strange piercing eyes, and a frail form. He was some "old writer" who had been wintering in the Lebanon and the ship had picked him up at Beirut.

When he collapsed and died over the breakfast table, there was the usual flurry. He was alone. Hurried consultations ended in the inevitable decision that he should be buried at the next port of call.

Upheaval

He was buried in Tunis last week—but not before distant relatives in Tennessee, U.S.A., had frantically cabled the Foreign Office about one Dr. Gerald Brosseau Gardner, aged 80, self-confessed witch, keeper of the museum of witchcraft at Castletown, Isle of Man, and author of books on witchcraft.

And when news of his death reached Britain there was a tremendous upheaval throughout every mysterious "witch coven," for Dr. Gardner was an unofficial, but tremendously powerful leader of the thousands of devotees to witchcraft here.

He was the man I heard mentioned many times during my investigations last Autumn into witchcraft in Britain to-day.

Thousands of Manx tourists met him—for he charged a shilling a head to visitors looking over Witch Mill at Castletown. They goggled at the collection of bones, charms, and "evil eyes" and instruments of torture connected with the great European purge of witches in the Middle Ages.

They heard Dr. Gardner (Doctor of Philosophy and

DR. GARDNER

Doctor of Literature) proclaim the virtues of the "old faith—older than Christianity" and heard him vow that he was a master of "white witchery."

The people of Castletown knew him only as a recluse; who suddenly came to them in 1946. Which by other records was the year he became a witch after 40 years as a customs officer in Malaya. And there are some who remember him in Liverpool.

But in England I knew him as a power—a leader of witches, who toured the country attending the secret meetings of the witches; advising and arbitrating on disputes.

Mrs. Eleanor Bone, a self-confessed witch of Trinity-road, Balham, London, told me: "The death of Dr. Gardner has shocked us all

deeply. There have been discussions as to who should take his place in our craft.

"I am the leader of a coven here in Balham, and I have talked with my counterparts in Sheffield and St. Albans. I anticipate that I will take over Dr. Gardner's role."

Quarrels

"His rise in our craft was almost an accident. But his personality and knowledge made him acceptable in all quarters, except in Scotland.

"Our intention now is to form a central committee of English witches, and I shall probably be voted the liaison officer between all covens."

Great debates — and quarrels—among witches open and secret are raging because of the death of Dr Gardner.

He took many secrets with him to the grave. But the upsurge in witchcraft in Britain which he lived to see is continuing—and even his death may well be accompanied by a further spurt.

An article by the *News of the World* on February 1964, about Gardner passing away onboard the ship, *The Scottish Prince,* whilst returning from wintering in sunnier climes. *Courtesy of Melissa Harrington and Melissa Seims.*

Alex Sanders

Founder of the Alexandrian Tradition

Helped to bring Awareness to Witchcraft

"If you don't talk about witchcraft, you will never banish forever the prejudice which surrounds it. And if you aren't prepared to be unorthodox, the Craft will stagnate and perish."

~said during an interview with
Men Only magazine, 1973

Renowned for establishing the Alexandrian Tradition, he is a controversial figure in witchcraft's recent history. Proclaiming himself the "King of Witches" Alex Sanders picked up where Gerald Gardner left off. Constantly in the media for his exploits and outrageous personality to his close confidants and initiates, he was a kind man with a tongue-in-cheek sense of humor. Born June 6ᵗʰ, 1926, and the eldest of six children, Sanders birth name was Orrel Alexander Carter, his father Harold Carter was a music hall entertainer who battled with alcoholism most of his life. The name Sanders came to Alex when his father decided to pick up and move the family to Grape Street in Manchester, England.

There are several varied accounts as to Alex's initial introduction to the Old Religion. The most famous is that printed in the book called *King of The Witches* by June John. Throughout his younger years, Alex suffered with bouts of tuberculosis; seeking a positive healing environment, the family would often take trips to visit his grandmother, lovingly called Grandma Bibby, in Wales. Alex claimed that one day he walked upon his grandmother performing a pagan rite, there and then she swore him to secrecy and initiated him into the Craft saying:

> One evening in 1933, when I was seven, I was sent round to my grandmother's house for tea. For some reason, I didn't knock at the door as I went in, and was confronted by my grandmother, naked, with her grey hair hanging down to her waist, standing in a circle drawn on the kitchen floor.

Sanders' grandmother was a hereditary witch, descendant of the Welsh Chieftain Owain Glyndŵr who was the last Welshman to hold the title of Prince of Wales and led a bloody revolt against England for the better part of the late 14ᵗʰ century and early 15ᵗʰ century. Glyndŵr, was also the last person to call himself "King of the Witches" or so Sanders believed, a title which Alex himself later took on. Alex continued to learn under his grandmother the rites, rituals, and beliefs of the Old Ways. He absorbed the information like a sponge. Due to his lineage, he was a natural psychic. He learned from his grandmother the art of "scrying." Just prior to Bibby's death, amidst the Blitz of WWII, Alex was given the second and third degree initiations which involved ritual sex. He also claimed that his grandmother gave him her *Book of Shadows* from which to copy notes and study.

Gardenarian High Priestess Patricia Crowther gives a different variation based on letters she received from Sanders in 1961. He stated in the letters that he felt a deep connection to the occult and had experiences of a psychic nature. But aside from that, he made no real mention of his grandmother. Then in an interview in 1962, he said that he had been initiated for a year and was involved in a coven led by a woman from Nottingham. The story about his grandmother would later be corroborated by his future wife and High Priestess Maxine Sanders.

Around the age of 21, Alex got a job as an analytical chemist. There he met his first wife, Doreen. She detested his spiritual beliefs and "odd practices." They had two children together but separation was inevitable; they divorced when Alex was 26. During an interview with the *Manchester Evening Chronicle* in 1962, in which Sanders was initiating a new member of his coven. He talked about how his religious system ruined his marriage:

> Our marriage went to the rocks almost overnight. My wife objected to me worshipping in the nude, as we do on occasions, because there are three women in my coven. But I have no regrets. I am a heathen and practising witchcraft is all important to me.

The reporters were led blindfolded to the ritual site, when they were finally allowed to remove the blindfolds, they discovered a "dead man" in the center of a circle; across him lay a sword. Sanders intoned:

> The "dead man" on the ground is now a witch. When he rises, he will be a man born again, with the powers to perform magic.

Sanders was strict on the reporters, never once allowing them to look directly upon the ritual, and never revealing the name of the "dead man" no matter how much the reporter pushed. At the end of the article, it seems the reporter had decided to get some opinions from the local ministry. They each concurred that what Alex was doing was pure rubbish.

Rev. C. A. Shaw of the Ambrose Church, Pendleton, Salford said:

> From the description you have given me of the midnight initiation, I would say that this is the type of thing I can imagine might have taken place in Lancashire in the 16th century. I think there is a strong psychological influence behind the people who practise witchcraft. They are children who have not grown up and are looking for an outlet.

The regret, anguish, feeling of isolation, and rejection was a turning point for Sanders. He left the path of the Goddess for a short time and began to follow the left-hand path. It is believed that during this time Sanders began using magic in order to secure wealth and power. He also supposedly cast a fertility spell as a way of vengeance against his ex-wife Doreen. According to Maxine when Doreen remarried she ended up with three sets of twins!

During this period, Alex whether due to his spell work or natural charm began attracting people who were paying for his lifestyle and media attention. Involved in Satanic ritual and Abra-melin magical systems he curried the media's favor. He talked about his experiences in the book, *Man Myth and Magic*:

> I made a dreadful mistake in using black magic in an attempt to bring myself money and sexual success. It worked all right — I was walking through Manchester and I was accosted by a middle-aged couple who told me that I was the exact double of their only son, who had died some years previously. They took me into their home, fed and clothed me, and treated me as one of the family. They were extremely wealthy, and in 1952, when I asked them for a house of my own, with an allowance to run it on, they were quite happy to grant my wishes. I held parties, I bought expensive clothes, I was sexually promiscuous; but it was only after a time that I realised I had a fearful debt to pay.

During this time Alex slept with both men and women without discretion—it was a particularly dark period. Soon he noticed the consequences of his actions in using selfish magic when one of his

HIGH PRIEST PERFORMS INITIATION AT MIDNIGHT

● After hearing rumours of strange Black Masses and witchcraft rites a "Saturday Chronicle and News" team went out to investigate. Last night, in a dark glade in the Cheshire countryside not far from Manchester, they attended the midnight initiation of a witch. On the left, blindfold and with their hands tied behind their backs, are Stan Royle, picture editor Jack Abell, and reporter David Duffy.

Manchester Evening Chronicle & News. September 15th 1962.

Amazing black magic rites on Cheshire hillside

'DEAD MAN" COMES TO LIFE, JOINS WITCHES

SHOCK 'CHRONICLE-NEWS' PROBE: CLERGY ATTACK

By DAVID DUFFY

FOR more than 15 fantastic minutes I sat blindfold, with my hands tied behind my back, and listened to the chant of a high priest as he initiated a witch into his coven.

Burning incense penetrated the midnight air and a chill wind swept the hillside at Alderley Edge, the famous Cheshire beauty spot. It was the "Festival of the Full Moon."

Only feet from where I was sitting—the very spot where the Wizard of Alderley practised his ancient cult centuries ago—was a magic circle surrounded by lighted candles, shielded from the wind with ferns.

In the centre of the magic circle lay a man purporting to be a "dead man." He was swathed in a white sheet, his face covered by a golden mask.

On his chest lay a sword, wand, and a thigh bone said to be that of a Knight Templar. Near by the head of a steel spear pierced the ground.

This was the amazing scene I saw when finally the high priest —36-year-old Alex Sanders—gave the order for my blindfold to be removed.

Clouds cast eerie shadows as Sanders said: "The 'dead man' on the ground is now a witch. When he rises he will be a man born again, with the powers to perform magic."

I challenged Sanders, who I can reveal has been practising witchcraft rituals on the Edge for 12 months, to reveal the initiate's identity.

He refused, "to protect him from any ridicule from his family and friends," he said.

The vow of allegiance

EARLIER, in company with photographer Stan Royle and picture editor Jack Abell, we had gone to the secret rendezvous at Alderley Edge.

Before the ceremony and in

ALDERLEY EDGE

order to see what was going on, we had to agree first to be blindfolded.

Sanders told us: "You will be able to listen to the rituals, but because they are secret we cannot allow you to witness them."

Even our hands were tied in case we were tempted to pull away the blindfolds and see what Sanders and his friends were up to.

During the "ceremony" Sanders, who described himself as "High Priest" spoke in a barbaric tongue. Bells were rung and the initiate repeated a vow of allegiance to the cult.

Then, after their gods were summoned from the four points of the compass, the new witch received his "magic tools"—the knife, a sword, a wand, and a spearhead.

Suddenly it was over. The initiate rose and lit a cigarette.

Then Sanders talked of how he sacrificed his marriage to practise witchcraft.

Power to cast spells

"OUR marriage went on the rocks almost overnight. My wife objected to me worshipping in the nude, as we do on occasions, because there are three women in my coven.

"But I have no regrets. I am a heathen, and practising witchcraft at all important to me. We do perform magic and have the power to cast spells, but we do no harm to anyone."

Sanders, an odd-job man in a

▲ Turn to Back Page

● On a slope at Alderley Edge a "dead man" takes part in a witchcraft initiation ceremony . . . dressed in white, wearing a golden mask with pictures of a god and goddess at his head and feet, and a sword, spearhead, and bone of a Knight Templar on and near his "body."

An article by David Duffy for the *Manchester Evening Chronicle and News*, September 15, 1962. *Courtesy of Melissa Harrington and Melissa Seims.*

● *Candles burn around the magic circle as High Priest Alex Sanders performs a phase of the initiation ceremony to make a "dead man" a witch. In the background the Edge.*

● *Part of the "opening of the mouth" ceremony on the "dead man" as High Priest Alex Sanders bends to say magic words.*

WITCHES' CEREMONY

▲ *Continued from Page 1*

Manchester library, lives in lodgings in Oldham Road, Newton Heath.

He added: "Through our cult, which has its origin 5,000 years ago, we try to seek a peaceful mind. I have been a witch since I was seven, my grandmother was High Priestess and she initiated me."

On New Year's Day, the "Festival of the Yule," Sanders, who now has 10 witches in his coven, says he plans to marry his "High Priestess," a 32-year-old woman from Nottingham.

"We would be married by ancient ritual," he said.

Back to the sixteenth century

AFTER reading this report, the Rev. C. A. Shaw, vicar of St. Ambrose Church, Pendleton, Salford to-day attacked witchcraft and said: "The Church of England would say immediately that witchcraft is complete and utter nonsense.

"From the description you have given me of the midnight initiation I would say that this is the type of thing I can imagine might have taken place in Lancashire in the 16th century.

"I think there is a strong psychological influence behind the people who practise witchcraft. They are children who have not grown up and are looking for an outlet."

The Rev. J. A. Dean, minister of Bramhall Congregational Church, said: "I feel the practising of witchcraft is misguided. It may be a modern way of achieving a new sensation, but their feelings have run away with their reasoning."

A Stretford Roman Catholic priest said: "The practice is stupid and in these modern times I cannot see any sense in it."

Part two of the article by David Duffy for the *Manchester Evening Chronicle and News*, September 15, 1962. *Courtesy of Melissa Harrington and Melissa Seims.*

lovers committed suicide, then his sister was wounded in an accidental shooting and diagnosed with terminal cancer. Alex blamed himself for the lives of these two women, and dedicated himself to teaching the craft, not using it for selfish reasons.

He talks about the personal tragedies and consequences in *Men Only* magazine:

> **Men Only:** *Black magic brought you fame and fortune, but it also brought you personal tragedy.*

> **Sanders:** *One of the girls I introduced to sex and perversion commit-ted suicide, and I'd really rather not talk about it even now. I had to give evidence at the inquest, and I shall never be able to forget the contemptu-ous stares of the others present. My parents cut me off. They had no idea that I was a witch and employing black magic, nor were they aware of my manner of living, but they sensed intuitively that I hadn't come into money by honest means. My poor mother even tried to commit suicide. Then I fell madly in love with a man. I followed him round Manchester for a year, not daring to speak to him, and when it all finally happened, we became lovers. Unfortunately, he suspected that, my sister Joan was really a girlfriend, and nothing I could do or say could convince him otherwise, so great was his sense of jealousy.*

> *The three of us had a terrible row in the front seat of his car, and before I knew what was happening, I heard a terrible explosion and saw a blinding flash of light. He had fired a pistol at me, and the bullet ricocheted around the inside of the car, going straight through my sister, and finally ending up in my shoulder. Joan had over a hundred stitches and nearly died. In fact, it did kill her because she never really recovered from that, and I am sure the bullet wounds caused the cancer from which she eventually died a terrible death after six months of suffering. That was the last straw. I gave up the house and the wealth and went through a period of purification.*

As he worked more with the Abra-melin, Alex began getting messages from angelic beings, one of them appeared to him and guided him to get a job at the John Ryland's Library in Manchester, England. There he found an original copy of the *Key of King Solo-mon*. He "borrowed" the book by taking it apart a couple of pages at a time. Alex was eventually caught in his destruction of the book, but no charges were ever brought against him; the library merely asked that the book be returned in whole. Needless to say he did lose that job.

Alex Sanders the Healer

Professing the ability to heal, one of Alex's first cases was actually that of his daughter. His wife at the time, Doreen, was in dry labor with their daughter Janice, the doctors did not think there was anything they could do for the infant. Her left foot was twisted backwards; the doctors had figured they would have to work with Janice on this when she reached her teens. Michael, one of Alex's familiars, told him to anoint the foot with warm olive oil, after doing this Alex turned his daughter's foot straight. It stayed and Janice had no problems except for the occasional almost arthritic like ache in cold and damp weather, which would cause a slight limp. Aside from healing the twisted leg, Alex said he was able to get rid of warts by wishing them to go to someone else, that he helped one woman with cystitis by laying his hands on her and willing the illness away. It is also believed that he had the ability to abort fetuses merely by pointing at the stomach and willing the child back to the Divine Source. He never doubted the power of pointing a finger; he felt he cured most people using this method. He also is believed to have cured a woman of cancer by laying his hands on her for three days and three nights pouring healing energy into her body.

Alex and The Gardenarians

While trying to move his way into Crowther's Gardenarian Coven, Alex had the idea to get witchcraft into the media. This was Sanders' first real brush with publicity. It worked, but had a couple of negative side effects, one of which being his rejection for admission into the coven. In the early sixties, especially in England, there were so many prejudices, Crowther thought that Sanders was courting trouble and wanted no part of it. Alex did eventually get into a Gardenarian coven; he was initiated to the first degree by Medea, unfortunately the coven dissipated within a year.

He continued to join a variety of covens and eventually gained his third degree by a priestess called Sylvia Tatham. She was an initiate in Crowther's coven and would later work with Maxine (Alex's future wife). Alex assumed position of High Priest in Sylvia's coven; Sylvia became High Priestess of New Zealand. Many believe that Alex Sanders got all of his information from Gerald Gardner's *Book of Shadows* after a trip to the Isle of Man.

NUDE WITCH CULT

Contrary to popular belief the word witch can be applied to both men and women. It stems from the Ancient Saxon Wica, meaning **Wise One**. The religion is based on the laws of nature, since primitive people were only concerned with rural occupations such as hunting and agriculture.

Briefly, the beliefs of the Witches are that everything in nature has a positive and a negative force. Hence the God is always thought of as wearing horns on his head to represent the virile and productive force in nature. The Goddess is thought of as the passive, or negative force and is the Eternal Mother, the Womb of Nature from whence all life springs and to which all life must return, even to the end of time.

Wica is a Matriarchal cult, woman being identified with the moon and its twenty-eight day cycle. As the Moon's power waxes and wanes so does the fertility cycle of woman wax and wane. The Goddess wears the symbol of the moon upon her brow. She was also known as the Queen of Heaven which is one of the titles of the Virgin Mary of Christianity. This may be one of the reasons why Christians who become interested in Wica find it easy to accept the religion. They are also not required to sever their connections with the Christian faith. And they may leave Wica at any time since nothing is done to prevent them, and no pressures are brought to bear.

Today witchcraft is not illegal in England. Unfortunately the religion had to be practised in great secrecy to prevent persecution. This has caused many stories of sex orgies, Voodoo satanism and black magic to be spread abroad. But perversions such as these are not encouraged by Wica which takes the same stand as Catholics, Protestants and Jews in this matter. As a matter of fact, a witch carries out the same function as a priest or a rabbi when he is invested with power and authority at his ordination. The Goddess says in Her 'Charge': "And mine also is joy on earth for my law is Love unto all beings." Jesus Christ says the same thing in different words: "Love Thy Neighbor."

In Manchester there are three covens of witches. Each coven has thirteen members. They come from all classes of society from the high to the low—working men and women and professional people as well. In one of the covens there are two policemen, and there are several priests of the Christian faith. The Elder of the Wica is a 39-year-old divorcee, Alexander Sanders, who is recognized as the leader of all the witches in the United Kingdom. He was inducted into the religion by his grandmother when he was eight. One day he was told by his mother that she would be out of her home when he came out of school. So he must go to his grandmother and she would call for him when she returned.

Alec went to his grandmother's home and walked in through the back door, unannounced, to find her naked in her living room practising the ancient religion of Wica. She initiated him as soon as he was old enough to understand the meanings. He has been a practising witch ever since.

He married, but his wife could not understand him because she

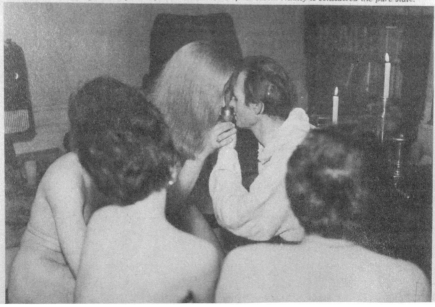

Visitors come regularly to the flat of "elder" Alex Sanders, some to seek advice, some to join the witches. Here a wine sipping ceremony takes place with members of the coven. Nudity is considered the pure state.

An article called "England's Nude Witch Cult" which appeared in the American publication *Swank* in March 1966. *Courtesy of Melissa Harrington and Melissa Seims.*

Left: Alex Sanders uses a "Hand of Glory" (human hand cut off a body hanging on the gallows) as a candle base as he casts a spell on a witch-hating neighbor. He made a wax figure of the woman, stuck a pin in her mouth, tied rope around the body. Though actually no hurt was caused, Sanders said the spell worked. Right: Kneeling before "elder" to receive blessing.

was not a member, and they eventually parted. He has amazing powers and told me within a few minutes of meeting, that I had an aura of America about me. He wanted to know if I was an American. I told him that I wasn't, but that I had just returned one week previously from New York.

The High Priest of the Coven that I visited is a magnetic young man called Paul King, a 22-year-old clerk who works for the Dunlop Rubber Company in the Manchester office. I also met Maxine Morris, tall blonde, 19-year-old priestess of the coven who is a shorthand typist, Jeanne Steven, a 19-year-old student, Diane Bradford who is the assistant matron of a nursing home, and Keith Johns, an engineer in his early twenties. They allowed me to photograph some of the rites and ceremonies of witchcraft—first of all at the Wizard's Stone at midnight, high on Alderley Edge, a crag with a knife edge not far from Manchester, a traditional meeting place of witches from the middle ages. Later we went to one of the temples in a house on the outskirts of Manchester and photographed other ceremonies. Certain rituals could not be photographed because I was not a member of Wica, but what I have recorded will give you some idea of the cult of witchcraft as practised in 20th Century Manchester.

Of course, there is still some persecution of witches. For instance, when her landlord found out that Maxine Morris was a witch, he made her leave her flat at very short notice. Some of the neighbors of Mr. Sanders have reported him and his activities to the police, but on investigation they have reported that there is nothing that they can do, since Mr. Sanders is a very law abiding citizen. Mr. Sanders says that he has now stopped his neighbor from causing any more trouble by a secret Wica method, which he demonstrated to me. He is certain that there will be no more action on her part. He has, however, been kidnapped and taken blindfolded in a car and beaten because of his beliefs. But he was able to use his powers to control his kidnappers and escaped from them.

He demonstrated his amazing powers to me during our visit to Alderley Edge. After the pictures were taken I was packing my equipment. One of the heads of my flash guns was loose. It fell to the ground and bounced towards the fissure which is the opening to the Wizard's Cave. The ground slopes towards the edge of the fissure and as my piece of equipment slithered downwards, I knew I had lost it down the fissure. But it stopped right on the edge. I looked up across the gaping mouth of the fissure and there saw Alexander Sanders staring at the flash head. When he saw me glance up, he said, "I didn't want you to lose that, so I stopped it for you. It's not damaged is it?"

Coincidence? Maybe. And then again, maybe not.　　THE END

Maxine Morris in her everyday clothes. Witchcraft isn't illegal, but landlady made Maxine move because of the cult.

Swank . . . . .

Part two of the article called "England's Nude Witch Cult" which appeared in the American publication *Swank* in March 1966. *Courtesy of Melissa Harrington and Melissa Seims.*

Many people believe that Alex Sanders named the tradition after himself, but Maxine Sanders tells a different story. The tradition was actually named after the ancient library of Alexandria; the Sanders saw it as the first place where people tried to bring worldly knowledge and wisdom together in one location. The name came about when Stewart Farrar (a student of Maxine and Alex's) was writing the book *What Witches Do*. One day, Stewart asked what witches who were initiated via their covens should be called; after much discussion, he came up with "Alexandrian" which both Alex and Maxine rather liked. Before this time they had been very happy to be called witches, Maxine had said.

Communication After Death

Jimahl di Fiosa hails from New England and is an Alexandrian witch. He was initiated into this branch of the craft in 1988 and considered it a major turning point in his life. He has devoted himself to the preservation of the craft for future generations.

In 1999, a book came out that touched many; that book was *Voices in the Forest* detailing one Alexandrian coven's experiences with a Ouija Board and the messages that came through. Many believe that the spirit speaking to the coven was the "King of the Witches" himself. Jimahl, who had never met Alex, could neither confirm nor deny that it was.

In the beginning, the book was self-published, and then it was picked up by Harvest Shadows Publications. I love internet radio and evidently so does Jimahl, while looking up more about this author, I found a show he had been a guest on called "The Witchcrafting Podcast" in August of 2001. In it he speaks about the book, the creation, the messages, and the impact.

The group initially went out on a camping trip up in New Hampshire, but it seemed what was to be a simple time was turned into a powerful experience when someone took out the Ouija Board. A spirit claiming to be Alex Sanders came through.

"It seemed ridiculous to us that the spirit would claim to be Alex Sanders, but the spirit was so strong that he started to tell us things that only Alex Sanders would know," Jimahl had said during the conversation.

Jimahl also implied that the book was never actually intended to be published and that his coven went back and forth with what to do about the information they had received. Ultimately, Jimahl decided to put the session's contents into a book because he felt the messages that they relayed were too important to be ignored.

Farewell chuckle of king witch

"Brighton Evening Argus."

May 2nd, 1988.

ALEX SANDERS, the "King of the Witches", has died — but he had the last laugh on some of his critics.

A bizarre figure, he was often in the news, notably when he put a curse on a Bexhill Light Operatic and Dramatic Society production because his wife had a row with the musical director.

Major rows followed and a group of other witches eventually reversed the spell.

But in a deathbed revelation, Alex told friends it was all a publicity stunt and he had never cursed the show in the first place.

Alex, 61, of Church Road, St Leonards, died at St Helen's Hospital, Hastings. He had been suffering from lung cancer.

Although he was famous throughout the world among people involved in witchcraft, he died virtually alone.

Witch Kevin Carlyon, 29, of London Road, Bexhill, said Alex's crowning as King of the Witches caused dispute in the world of witchcraft and many believed he should not have the title.

He said there will be more arguments soon when the

Alexandrian Movement of Witches — named after Alex — holds discussions in a bid to crown his 16-year-old son Victor as the new king.

His former wife was concert pianist Gillian Sicka. Kevin said she forbade her children to have anything to do with the occult.

Alex Sanders claimed to have been initiated into witchcraft by his grandmother when he was just seven and he went on to run large covens.

Kevin said Alex was both a black witch and a white witch and did some good and some evil.

Occultists from all over the country are expected to attend his funeral, which is likely to be next week.

An article about Alex Sanders death in the Brighton *Evening Argus* May 2, 1988. *Courtesy of Melissa Harrington and Melissa Seims.*

Many must wonder why Alex would contact this group. Why not Maxine? Why not some of his other friends and confidants? Why this group of New England witches? Jimahl has his own theories. He says in the interview, "I don't believe there is anything special about us; I think that we were just listening."

After reading the book, I soon realized that the information contained within was not simply generic, these were specific messages, names, and a specific personality, a certain way of speaking, that were pure Alex Sanders. I can only say that because of all the research I have done on him – the interviews, both taped and written. It seems that once you get into the person, the entity that is Alex, it becomes an all-consuming need to find out more. So in reading this book, a chord was struck. Could the "King of the Witches" be so close?

Maxine Sanders had not yet heard of the book until a friend of Jimahl's sent it to her (without letting him know) and she later submitted a quote to the Alexandrian newsletter *The Guardian:*

> I was sent a book from America called *A VOICE IN THE FOREST*. I was prepared to be skeptical, as there have been so many false contacts with Alex. I worked with Alex in mediumistic circles for many years and knew his techniques well. The contact described within the book was so obviously true it gave me goose bumpts. After Alex's death, the rites of "sending forth" were performed …. (but) it would seem that Alex still had something to say, showing that some things never change."
>
> ~Maxine Sanders

Jimahl had procrastinated in sending Maxine the book because of his own vulnerabilities he told Karagan during the *Witchrafting* Podcast interview:

> I wasn't sure I wanted her to see because I believe the book is real, but obviously when you become vulnerable to where you're exposing the book, to somebody who knew Alex that intimately, you're going to find out rather quickly whether or not the person will validate the book or dismiss it.

After getting Maxine's approval, Jimahl saw it as the green light for really getting the book out to people, that for the skeptics out there he had validation, not just from Maxine but also from others who knew Alex. Although the book is by Jimahl di Fiosa it is really, a work of Alex Sanders, but it is by no means a biography. More, it is an instructional, a spiritual message, and a hope.

There are many things that Alex speaks about in the book, he talks about the nature of the gods and how we view God and Goddess and what this means to us. He talks about the afterlife and what it's like, and he addresses the process of reincarnation from his perspective. So there are many wonderful things but if you really look at it in its most basic terms the book really has one message and it's togetherness; it's a word that Alex used in his first communication. But I really think it is a message of unity a message of pagans. People who worship the Goddess, wiccans, must all start to look for things that will bind us together, that will bring us together instead of looking at things that make us different, that separate us.

Jimahl is currently working on a new book project entitled, *All the King's Children*. In it, he will interview people who were taught by Alex. "It's not about Alex but his legacy, the human legacy of Alex Sanders."

The Differences between Alexandrians and Gardenarians

I thought this would be a good place to point out some of the key differences between the two traditions. Yes, the Alexandrian tradition can be looked at as an offshoot of the Gardenarians. However, unlike the Gardenarians, the tradition that Alex Sanders created is more open to gays, lesbians, and transsexuals. Sanders viewed the male/female in a less concrete form; it seems that he saw both aspects in everyone, unlike in the Gardenarian tradition, which looks at the polarity of the fertility rituals in a much more strict fashion.

Alexandrian covens are sky clad optional depending on the wishes of the High Priestess or Priest. In the Gardenarians when working in a coven, they tend to cast circle, and call quarters with only the High Priestess, Priest, Summoner, and Maiden in circle, then a doorway is cut and the other ritualists are allowed inside.

Alexandrians view the athame as having a connection to air and the wand to fire whereas the Gardenarians view it in the opposite manner. Both are considered British Traditional Wicca, both have three degrees and both (for the most part) do not recognize self-initiations. Alexandrian is considered to be somewhat more eclectic, and take on the motto "if it works use it." Deity names also differ from the Gardenarian tradition, and the Alexandrian tradition incorporates Enochian magic and Kabbalah into their rituals.

Gavin Frost

Co-Founder of the Church and School of Wicca

Responsible for Recognition of Wicca

as a Valid Religion by the Federal Courts

"In the early days there was a great deal of excitement and dedication to Wicca."

~Gavin Frost
(during an interview) Pagannews.com

Founder of The Church and School of Wicca, Gavin Frost was born in Staffordshire, England in 1930. His Welsh grandfather had established a successful canning business, where the family members all worked and took part in some form or another. After the death of Gavin's grandfather (date not found), he was sent by family members to a respected boarding school to further his education. While Gavin was attending school, he excelled in mathematics and physics, and in 1949, became enrolled into King's College at the University of London to further his studies in these areas. In 1953, Gavin received his Bachelors degree and then not too long after received his Doctorate in math.

Thomas Lethbridge, who had at the time worked as a lab assistant at the College, was intrigued in the occult studies. Gavin decided to join Thomas's group of like-minded individuals. Right after the Witchcraft Act had been repealed in 1951, like many other individuals and witches, the group of four men decided to get initiated into a coven, but to do that, they needed a resource.

A former student of the College had joined a coven in Penzance, England. Once the contact was made, the coven members gave instructions to the initiates. They were blindfolded and taken to a sacred place called Nine Maidens Circle or Boskednan Stone Circle in Cornwall. As part of the ceremony, each initiate went through a ritual and then was cut by a blade on the wrist as part of the initiation.

Gavin had graduated with honors from King's College; he had now a Bachelor of Science degree in Mathematics. He then moved on, gaining yet another Doctorate in Physics and Mathematics from his thesis work with the Department of Atom Energy. All this lead Gavin to a career in the Aerospace industry. Gavin still had a passion for knowledge on religious studies and different types of witchcraft, such as German witchcraft. Later, during Gavin's still youthful years while traveling due to his job, he joined a coven, or some might say a group of Zauberers (a group of German magicians).

Meanwhile Gavin's first marriage seemed to be falling apart, because of all the traveling he had to do for his employer. While returning to California in 1968, Gavin had started writing a book called *Pagans of Stonehenge*. When he went to work one day to ask one of the secretaries to type and edit his work for him, it was the beginning of Gavin and Yvonne's (the secretary!) life together. It was not too soon before the love began to grow between them as well as their love for religion and magical studies.

In 1968, Gavin and Yvonne moved to St. Louis, Missouri, where together they founded the first Church and School of Wicca. This school started out as a correspondence school through the mail, teaching many different subjects such as Witchcraft as a spiritual path, astral travel, and many different areas of psychic studies. In 1972, the school was given by law a religious tax-exempt status. Because of the step forward the Frosts had made, it changed the way the laws looked at Wicca as a recognized religion.

District Court Excerpts

With the above principles in mind the Court thinks that the Church of Wicca is clearly a religion for first amendment purposes: Members of the Church sincerely adhere to a fairly complex set of doctrines relating to the spiritual aspects of their lives and in doing so they have "ultimate concerns" in much the same way as followers of more accepted religions. Their ceremonies and leader structure, their rather elaborate set of articulated doctrines, their belief in the concept of another world, and their broad concern for improving the quality of life for others gives them at least some facial similarity to other more widely recognized religions. While there are certainly aspects of Wiccan philosophy that may strike most people as strange or incomprehensible, the mere fact that a belief may be unusual does not strip it of Constitutional protection. Accordingly, the Court concludes that the Church of Wicca, of which the plaintiff IS a sincere follower, is a religion for the purpose of the free exercise clause."

~Page 596 617 Federal Supplement

Federal Appeals Excerpts

[I]" In determining whether the Church of Wicca is a religion protected by the free exercise clause of the first amendment, the district court considered whether the Church occupies a place in the lives of it's members "parallel to that filled by the orthodox belief in God" in religions more widely accepted in the United States. (United States v Seeger, 380 U.S. 163,166,85 S.Ct. 850,854,13 L.Ed.2d 733 (1964)}

The district court found that members of the Church of Wicca "adhere to a fairly complex set of doctrines relating to the spiritual aspects of their lives." These doctrines concern ultimate questions of human life, as do the doctrines of recognized religions.{ See Africa v Pennsylvania, 662 F 2d 1025,1032(34 Cir. 1982); International Society for Krishna Consciousness, Inc. v Barber,650 F. 2d 430,440(24 Cir. 1981); Malnak v Yogi, 592 F.2d 197,208, (34 Cir. 1979) (Adams, J., Concurring)} (Text not included here)

We agree with the district court, 617 F.Supp 592 (1985) that the Church of Wicca occupies a place in the lives of it's members parallel to that of more conventional religions. Consequently, it's doctrine must be considered a religion.

Gavin and his wife, Yvonne, made an impact for the wiccans all over the world because of their fight for religious rights as wiccans and fought to make Wicca a known religion so that the everyday individual, individuals in the different branches of the military, and even inmates, could practice their Wiccan path. (The Frosts wrote a section of the Washington's State Prison inmate's handbook, called "State of Washington Prisoner's Handbook for Wicca.")

3

Twenty-First Century Witchcraft

Being a Solitary

Being a solitary comes from one of two reasons: neccessity or choice. With covens, it is always a choice to join, but sometimes being a solitary is not a matter of choosing the path but an inability to find those like-minded souls around you. I can say only one thing, thank goodness for the internet. With the widespread of cyberspace, people are literally creating internet covens and study groups to trade ideas so those interested can keep the freedom of being a solitary while still interacting with those who understand one's love of Deity and preference of worship.

There are a number of reasons why being a solitary is a positive thing. Most solitaries end up becoming eclectic witches if they are not of a family tradition. This is because they are allowed the freedom to explore. It also allows you to find your own personal power and connection with the Divine rather than having to develop a need for a group in order to create the same connection.

Also, the more people you have involved, the more likely that there is inevitable drama! As a solitary, you can seek your own peace and not have to worry about the distractions that come with meetings and other gatherings. For some, the structure of a coven can actually give a feeling of limitations; you are taught one way and you are expected to follow it until you leave the coven. This can give a feeling of being stifled. Being a solitary practitioner allows you to worship your Deities in whichever way you choose; if you're a day late with your Mabon ritual, the Gods don't mind, but a coven would.

Also, as a solitary you can be a part of a variety of circles, many new age and metaphysical stores offer open circles. As a solitary you can soak in the knowledge, other traditions, and information presented to you. Take what you will and leave the rest.

There are a couple of other reasons why the solitary path may be for you. Some people feel that if they join a coven they will be "outed" in one way or another to family and friends who may not look too kindly at the religion because they choose to remain ignorant. As a solitary, you can keep yourself safely tucked away in the "broom closet" until that time that you are ready to take the step forward and declare your religious affiliations.

For most solitary witches though, they feel that their connection with Deity is not one that is in need of being on display. They feel it is a private, personal, and profound experience when they conduct their rituals and they would rather not have a bunch of eyes staring at them.

Most of all, whether trying to make the choice of joining a coven or stay a solitary, you need to trust your intuition and listen closely to the Goddess and God. They will never steer you wrong.

Covens

"I realised that I had stumbled upon something interesting; but I was half-initiated before the word, 'Wica' which they used hit me like a thunderbolt, and I knew where I was, and that the Old Religion still existed. And so I found myself in the Circle, and there took the usual oath of secrecy, which bound me not to reveal certain things."

~Gerald Gardner,
The Meaning of Witchcraft, 1959

A grove of trees and a bunch of black-robed women circled round a cauldron beneath a full moon. That is the picture most people have in their minds when they think about a coven. During my studies into different religions, I have learned to paint a very different picture. There may be robes of black, sometimes purple, that is true; and yes, a cauldron may be present, as well as both women and men. However, I have seen gatherings outside and inside. At each gathering there is plenty of laughter and talk. They are not always somber affairs and do not expect to chant at every coven meeting. There is always something new to learn in a coven, new ideas being incorporated.

Many of the covens that I have attended have been Modern or Eclectic covens, drawing their inspiration from all over the pagan tree and its branches. Some covens prefer more traditional and structured atmospheres which include lineages, i.e., John Doe initiated by Lady Mary who was initiated by Lord Merlin. Many witches today have sought solitary paths, but still there are those who long for a place to belong, a place where the trading of philosophies and structured learning can occur.

However, what exactly is a coven; do you need one and why are they important?

What is a Coven?

A Coven is a structured group of like-minded individuals of the same tradition who meet on certain days and times for meetings, gathering of holiday celebrations and ceremonies of their worship.

These covens become an extended part of the initiate's family. Coven leadership varies depending on tradition and inclination; sometimes there will be just a high priestess or a high priest and priestess of the coven. Joining a coven is not for everyone; make sure this is what you truly need and want before wasting anyone's time.

Each coven has its own rules and regulations that each member must follow. How many members does a coven need to be considered a coven? It honestly depends, some covens only have three or four members and others have thirteen. If a coven becomes too large, then most likely it would branch off or make a "hive." In this case, a member of the coven who has reached the training of a high priestess or high priest would be the one to start this new offshoot.

It is accepted as being binding forever, and no initiate can take it lightly. She accepts wholeheartedly all the tenets of witchcraft—the acceptance of the Supreme Being, the knowledge that good and evil are equal parts of a human being, and that she must personally strive to outbalance evil with good. She must not debase the arts which she has been taught, and at all times she must be conscious of the need to be discreet, not only in her own life but with regard to any other members of the coven.

~Sybil Leek
Diary of a Witch (1969)

There are many positive benefits from joining a coven, such as those experienced by Macha Raven Mare, a Priestess in her rural community.

I truly enjoyed the freedom of the solitary eclectic path. During my time I created a beautiful relationship with Deity through my own unique rituals, devotions, and workings. Throughout this decade of self-exploration, I discovered that I was a very diverse witch whom did not like too much structure within my practices. I enjoyed the freedom of being a solitary, to explore different traditions on my own terms.

I got to live by my own set of ethics, although I always followed the Rede. There was a freedom in being accountable only to Deity and myself. Something was missing though, it was the feeling of interrelated group energy and love that is found within a spiritual family, those in which to share her passion, energy, and love for the path. I decided to set out and form a study grove, not technically a coven, but more so a place to trade ideas, learn and grow within our own spiritualities. A place of community and friendship, for people like me who sought and wanted to make connections, to share their love and passion for the Craft together. There was a great need for that feeling of connectedness; I soon realized I wasn't the only one yearning for it. I lead rituals, taught workshops, helped guide newcomers to the best sources of reference and learning. In the years following my leadership within the study grove, watching the members grow and evolve, I made connections with individuals who eventually brought to me an opportunity for Coven work.

I couldn't pass it up. Working within a coven was a much different experience, working with a group of people, losing the solitary status brought with it a different dynamic, but no less sacred. The coven I belong to is eclectic, thus allowing me to retain my own beliefs, while working harmoniously in a more structured environment. Coven work brings the opportunity of working with individuals who have a wide variety of wisdom, knowledge, and experiences that can be shared. Becoming one with group energy, and drawing upon group power, versus individual is very fulfilling. I feel complete with the sense of camaraderie within a coven, but I still believe that witches are a solitary at heart, sovereign unto themselves. We all come from a place of self-discovery; the Divine spirit resides within each one of us. We individually look to nature with wonder and love in our heart, but it is through community, friendship, and sharing that brings it all full circle for me.

How to Find and Join a Coven

With more technology at our finger tips today, finding a local group or coven is not that hard. The internet is such a huge resource for many of us and a wonderful way to connect with like-minded individuals and even covens have web pages now! You can find out all about their system of magick, and their way of being before you even send in an application. There are many *meet and greet* groups around most of the local towns and cities; these are free of charge and a great way to meet new people and make new friends. When you discover the coven that best fits your path and needs, most will allow the potential candidate to attend several of their coven meetings and introduce the coven members to the candidate. After a few meetings under your belt, the coven will most likely take a vote on the candidate's application or membership. This is a time for the candidate to also reflect on whether this coven is right or wrong for their needs. Ask yourself, does this coven follow my own belief systems? Is this coven going to bring me growth and understanding of the craft? Does my personality clash with other coven members? Really, think about the decision, because the coven members will be doing the same.

In today's society, we see many types of people and different types of covens or groups out there, some unfortunately are not a healthy choice for you to join. Mind you though, there are tons of great educational groups and covens out in the world today; just do your research before joining.

Now, what types of covens should an individual avoid joining? Never join any type of group or coven if their principles are not the same as yours. I know that sounds like common sense, but I have seen too many times those who are willing to bend their beliefs just to be accepted. If there are "power" trips going on within the coven, walk away very quickly and look for another more mature group or coven to join. If a coven leader demands sexual acts as an initiation into the coven, this is wrong and is NOT how a legit coven works. If the coven leader/leaders try to make sexual advances towards you, again not a group or coven I personally would want anything to do with. Quickly walk away and look elsewhere. Never give up family, friends, or money if a coven or coven leader asks an individual to do so as a requirement to come into the coven. This is not a "real" coven and reminds me more of a dangerous "cult" type of setting.

There are a few more issues to bring up, and you, as the seeker, need to watch out for during your search. No legit coven will allow the use of drugs among the members and or during the coven meetings or gatherings. I have to say up front, most covens do share or have some form of wine or alcohol during their celebrations and holidays. This is common within the covens, BUT if one does not drink alcohol; no leader or other coven member would ever force the alcohol issue on that person or have the person removed from the coven. The best thing you can do is research, research, research. There are a lot of people on the internet and around your area who most likely belong to covens and would be willing to answer questions.

Spells, Chants, and Rituals

Magick of the Elders

Song of the Witches

Double, double toil and trouble;
Fire burn and caldron bubble.
Fillet of a fenny snake,
In the caldron boil and bake;
Eye of newt and toe of frog,
Wool of bat and tongue of dog,
Adder's fork and blind-worm's sting,
Lizard's leg and howlet's wing,
For a charm of powerful trouble,
Like a hell-broth boil and bubble.
Double, double toil and trouble;
Fire burn and caldron bubble.
Cool it with a baboon's blood,
Then the charm is firm and good.

~William Shakespeare
Macbeth

Spell and Rituals

Here are some spells, chants, and rituals passed down from our elders of the craft. I have included some of Laurie Cabot's spells in this section because she is an elder of the craft.

The Invocation for Unity of Spirit

Thy present bounty, O limitless Goddess of infinite light, began with thy renewed revelation of thyself unto the peoples and nations of the earth! Thy mercy and compassion hath been made manifest unto those who hath completed the seventh circuit of life, death, and life again, and whom thou hast specifically chosen to open thy jeweled gates of knowledge. Thou hast touched the souls of some few women and men with the spark of primeval recognition at this, the beginning of the age. These few proclaim thee as the Everlasting and Transcendent Goddess of all things! These few declare, testify, and bear witness that this planet is as one nation, and that its peoples are all thy children from before all beginnings unto beyond all endings! Strengthen thou the souls of them who acknowledge thee, O Supreme Creatrix, and bless them who openly proclaim thee unto all as Ultimate Divinity! Blessed be, O Supreme Goddess, in all thy many names and manifold attributes!

~Sybil Leek

Invocation To Obtain Help

Thy love and compassion hath strengthened me, thrice-crowned Goddess of the Cosmos All. Thy guidance hath been a

From *The Book of Hallowe'en* by Ruth Edna Kelley 1919. Picture is called, "A Witches' Cauldron Table."

granite fortress set upon the mountain peak. Thy sacred law of life hath been a consecrated wall of jeweled flames protecting me. Yet in this moment and in this place I am in need of thy healing and comforting presence, O beloved Goddess of all good beginnings.

Be with me in the midst of my present difficulties. With thy hand of power and might, O merciful and compassionate Goddess of the Best and Good, direct me that I may remove, with thy help, the sorrows and afflictions which now surround me. Grant me the protection of the sanctified sword of thy truth, O beloved Goddess of the original primeval wisdom. In thee am I made powerful and confident. Thou art my aid and help, O Triple Goddess. Blessed be, O Supreme Goddess, in all thy many names and manifold attributes!

~Sybil Leek

The Bottle Spell

This is used as a neutralizing spell in case you are in any psychical harm or threatened.

    4 tablespoons frankincense or myrrh
    4 tablespoons black powered iron
    4 tablespoons sea slat
    4 tablespoons orris-root powder
    1 white candle
    1 bottle with a cork or lid
    mortar and pestle
    parchment paper
    black ink or black ballpoint pen
    black thread

Mix sea salt, orris-root powder and iron in a bowl. Cut a piece of parchment to fit inside the bottle and write on it with black ink,

I neutralize the power of (name) to do me any harm. I ask that this be correct and for the good of all. So mote it be.

Roll up the parchment, tie it with black thread to bind it, and place it into the bottle. Fill the bottle with the dry ingredients. Then take the white candle and, while turning the bottle counterclockwise, drip wax over the cork to seal it.

Secretly bury the bottle in a safe place where no person or animal will dig up the bottle. This spell is like a genie in a bottle, never unleash the cork or the power of the spell is broken.

~Laurie Cabot

A Spell for Success

This spell is to make a Business Profitable.

Take:

    1 tablespoon cloves
    1 tablespoon eyebright
    1 tablespoon mistletoe

Add a few drops of cinnamon oil to the above ingredients.

Now bind together the following ingredients:

    1 tablespoon orris root powder
    1 tablespoon frankincense
    1 teaspoon myrrh

Before mixing the ingredients together, it is important to charge the frankincense and myrrh to bind the spell.

Say the following out loud or to yourself:

I want my business to be profitable and successful.

Mix the ingredients now. Ask that the spell,

Be correct and for the good of many people. So mote it be.

Put the philter (potpourri) in a bowl, burn as incense over charcoal and/or carry in a bright gold magic bag to draw in the energy of the Sun. In addition, one could use a royal blue magic bag to draw in the energy of Jupiter, or an orange magic bag to draw in the energy of Mercury.

~Laurie Cabot

A Spell to Attract Wealth, Food, and Clothing

Take:

- 1 tablespoon angelica root or seeds
- 1 tablespoon yellow mustard seed
- 1 tablespoon mistletoe
- 1 tablespoon saffron
- 1 tablespoon aloe powder

To these ingredients, add the following:

- 10 drops of sweet orange oil
- 10 drops of sandalwood oil
- 10 drops of jasmine oil

Bind it all together with the following ingredients:

- 1 teaspoon gum mastic
- 1 tablespoon frankincense

Mix all the ingredients together and catalyze the intentions, say out loud or to yourself the following:

This spell is to assure that changes will bring gain and benefit to me. So mote it be. I ask that this spell be correct for the good of many people. So mote it be.

Carry this philter in a gold lame or black magic bag.

~Laurie Cabot

Chants

Charge of the Goddess

Listen to the words of the Great Mother, who was of old also called among men Artimis Astarte Diane: Melusine Aphrodite Cerridwen Dana Ariaurhod Bride. And by many other names.

At mine altars the youth of Lacedemon in Sparta made due sacrifice. Whenever ye have need of anything, once in the month, and better be it when the moon is full, then ye shall assemble in some secret place and adore the spirit of me who is queen of all witchery.

There shall ye assemble ye who are fain to learn all sorcery, Yet have not won it's deepest secrets: to these will I teach things that are yet unknown.

And ye shall be free from slavery. And as a sign that ye be really free, ye shall be naked in your rites. And ye shall dance; sing; feast; make music, and love, all in my praise. For mine is the ecstacy of the spirit: and mine also is joy on earth for MY law is love, unto all beings.

Keep pure your highest idea, strive ever toward it. Let naught stop you or turn you aside.

For mine is the secret door which opens upon the door of youth. And mine is the cup of the wine of life; and the cauldron of Cerridwen, which is the holy grail of immortality. I am the gracious goddess who gives the gift of joy unto the heart of man Upon earth I give the knowledge of the spirit eternal: And beyond death I give peace and freedom: and reunion with those who have gone before: nor do I demand sacrifice: for behold, I am the Mother of all living: and my love is poured out upon the earth.

Hear ye the words of the Star Goddess: She in the dust of whose feet are the hosts of heaven, whose body encircleth the universe. I who am the beauty of the green earth: and the white moon amongst the stars: and the mystery of the waters: and the desire of the heart of man call unto thy soul; arise and come unto me.

For I am the soul of nature who giveth life to the universe; from me all things proceed; and unto me all things must return; and before my face, beloved of gods and men, thine inmost divine self shall be enfolded in the rapture of the infinite. Let my worship be within the heart that rejoiceth: for behold: all acts of love and pleasure are my rituals: and therefore let there be beauty and strength, power and compassion, honor and humility, mirth and reverence within you.

And thou who thinkest to seek for me: Know thy seeking and yearning shall avail thee not, unless thou know the mystery; that if that which thou seekest thou findest not within thee, thou wilt never find it without thee: For behold — I have been with thee from the beginning: and I am that which is attained at the end of desire.

~Sybil Leek

The Witches' Chant

Darksome night and Shining Moon,
East, then South, then West, then North,
Harken to the Witches Rune:
Here come I to call thee forth.
Earth and Water, Air and Fire,
Wand and Pentacle and Sword,
Work ye unto my desire,
Harken ye unto my word.
Cords and Censer, Scourge and knife,
Powers of the Witches Blade,
Waken all ye into life,
Come ye as the Charm is made:
Queen of Heaven, Queen of Hell,
Horned Hunter of the Night,
Lend your power unto the Spell,
Work my will by Magic Rite.

If chant is used to reinforce a work already begun, end with this:

By all the power of land and sea,
by all the might of moon and sun,

What is my will—"So mote it be,"
What I do say—"It shall be done."

~*Gardnerian Book of Shadows*

Gerald Gardner's handmade sword; although never used in ritual, he made it in case any of his followers decided to "hive off" and needed one. *Courtesy of the Museum of Witchcraft on loan from Patricia Crowthers.*

Modern-Day
Spells, Rituals, and Chants

The Triple Goddess

Maiden of the waxing bow
Silver crescent hanging low
Primal Huntress, Running deer
Forests deep and shining spear,
Chant to her a rhyming boon
For all things new to come right soon

Mother, sea and fertiles ground,
Heavy moon so full and round
Warmth and life she doth bring,
To every sacred living thing
In the cold and maternal dark,
Look within the find spark.
Take a seed, and plant it deep.
Your heartfelt boon you shall reap

Ancient Crone dark and wise
Moonless night and ravens eyes
Cloak of Stars, Spiral around,
Torch lit shadows upon the ground
Hag of crossroads holds the key
To wisdom, rebirth and mystery
Above, Below, within and without
Hear her voice when ever in doubt

When and if you are in need

Look to the sacred blessed three

Seek her light, her wisdom and love.

Find her three faces in the moon above,

For the highest good and the power of three

In the Lady's name

So Mote it be

~Poem by Macha Raven Mare

I n this section I have included some wonderful spells, chants, and rituals from our modern witches, wiccans, and pagans of today. I am a grassroots kind of researcher and with so many active witches, wiccan, and pagans around us today, I couldn't resist tapping into them as a resource. Using their knowledge of the Craft, their spells and their poetry, I hope to show that they are everywhere and not just in the new age section at the bookstore. Through each of us, the words and teachings of the Great God and Goddess will remain alive for centuries to come because of individuals such as these.

&‌ *Please note: All material for the modern-day spells, rituals, and chants is original and may not be used in any form unless given by written permission by the authors.*

* Remember, no matter what type of spell or ritual one is performing be respectful and responsible. These spells and rituals will not make a person a witch, and never perform any type of magick if one is feeling in a negative mood. No matter how positive the spell or ritual may be, the outcome could be the opposite. *

"The Goddess walks by my side, I will have peace tonight.

Cerridwen weaver of stories and time protect me."

~Lady D.
Chant for Protection from Nightmares

Common Tools of The Craft.

To Protect Animals from Abuse

"If there is one thing, I despise more than anything else is the abuse of innocent animals. All of God's creatures need to be treated with love and respect, and that certainly includes those in the animal kingdom. Unfortunately, we cannot be there to protect all of the unfortunate creatures who may suffer at the hands of cruel and heartless humans. However, we can take action against animal cruelty, whether it be on a personal or global level, with the following spell."

You will need:

> A purple candle
> Frankincense Incense
> Patchouli oil
> A quartz crystal
> A sharp pin

With the pin, etch your intentions into the candle.

Anoint the candle with the oil and repeat the following incantation:

> *Protect all abused creatures from violence and pain*
> *Protect them from those who are filled with disdain*
> *Protect them from anger and hardship and greed*
> *Protect them from those who lie and mislead*
> *May Karma take over with lightning speed*
> *And stop the insanity*
> *Let these creatures be freed*
> *So Mote It Be.*

This spell is strongest when done on the New Moon.

~Marla Brooks
Author, *Animal Spells and Magick*

House Blessing

The idea behind a House Blessing is simple. You are moving any energy out of the area that has been left by the previous occupants, even if those were builders, and replacing it with divine energy that you ask for. You are setting the foundation of energy, and harmony in the space for you and your family to walk into, as well as asking for blessings for the future.

This ritual is of course written from the perspective of Shamanism, but all religions have some form of similar ceremony. You can take these steps and alter it slightly to fit your personal beliefs and practices, and use tools you feel comfortable with.

Many craft stores now carry smudge sticks, large imitation eagle feathers, scented oils, and everything you'll need for this ritual. If you can't find items listed here, there are many online stores who offer these products. You might also try finding a pagan shop in your area through a search at AvatarSearch.com or Witchvox.net. But these items are not set in stone, you can improvise to items that you feel more comfortable with that support your own personal belief system.

Before you begin, gather the items you'll need. You will prepare 2 small altars, one outside the house and one inside the house to hold the objects you'll need. Gather together:

Outside the House

If possible – If your home is an apartment or a place where you can't leave an altar outside, set the altar just inside the door.

A white candle.
A lighter or book of matches.
Sage and cedar smudge, if you can find it. If not sandlewood, incense will suffice. Non-Pagans might prefer Frankincense and Mir, which are a common combination in their rituals for cleansing spaces. But um...if you've never smelled Frankincense and Mir; you might stick with the sage and cedar.
A large feather.

For Inside the House
Place a small altar just inside the door to hold:

A holder for the sage and cedar smudge stick, or the incense you chose to use.

For the Protection

You'll need to have prepared a potion for this. See the Rose Shield potion for instructions.

IF you do not have time, or don't feel you can make the potion yourself, purchase a small bottle of Rose oil (about 2 ounces), and a larger glass container to hold a little mixture you're going to have to make. You can get these from your local craft store. When you return home, pour half the contents of the rose oil into the bottle. Tear up 4 or 5 rose pedals and add them to the bottle. Boil some tap water, and fill up the bottle. Now you have a quick protection potion.

Some people like to go all out and also purchase a garland made of roses to hang around the door way of their home. It's a beautiful idea, but can be costly. I've also conducted House Blessing rituals where the owners purchased a dozen roses and placed one rose before each door that leads outside, and upon each window sill.

Yellow or Gold taper candle.

For the Blessing

Lavender Incense

Lavender taper candle.

The New Home Ritual

Clearing

Creating your space, begins with you. Before you can begin any spiritual work, be it a simple mediation or full blown ceremony complete with pomp and circumstance, YOU must be prepared. Being Grounded and Balanced before any spiritual work is essential to both your intent and the effectiveness of you work. So take a few moments to read the process for Grounding and Balancing For Ritual Work.

Lighting the Altar Candle Outside

Starting outside. The altar is placed just before the front door facing the door. Give yourself some room to walk around the altar to enter the door way. About 4 feet before should be fine. If you can't set the altar outside, you might use a small TV tray that can be easily moved and place it "in" the door way with the door open. While you stand outside to begin the process, you can move the altar inside and close the door when it comes time to enter the home.

Some people like to perform this ritual with a partner or friend who can help keep your home safe while you're walking through this process. For instance, you don't want the outside altar candle blowing over and starting a fire, while you're walking through the house. So

your partner can standby and make sure it's safe, or once you enter the home to clear the energy, they can carry the outside altar to just inside the door way and insure it's securely placed in a safe manner.

1. Begin with lighting your altar candle. This is the white candle you selected in your preparations.

   Close your eyes and imagine a flame being lit within your own body.
   Imagine your spiritual essence, lighting a flame in your solar plexus. This is your divine light, the spirit within you that will provide the energy to the wick of your candle and the work ahead.
   With each breath you take, imagine the flame inside your being growing stronger and brighter, until it fills your entire body with its warmth and bright light.
   Open your eyes, take the matches/lighter in hand and light the wick of your candle.
   Say something like:

   Great Spirits,
   I (or we), state your name(s),
   bring to light this flame of fire,
   to clear, cleanse and protect my
   home from the muck and mire.

   {pick up the smudge stick and present it to the divine forces}

2. Place the smudge over the candle's flame and set it afire. While the smudge is still on fire, call upon your God/Goddess of choice. (If you're not pagan, you can easily call upon your own God). Say something like:

> *Great Spirits, (God/Goddess name)*
>
> *Through divine love and light,*
>
> *I call upon your great might,*
>
> *To open this space for your noble charge.*

3. Holding the smudge in your left hand and the feather in your right, step toward your door, blow out the flames of the smudge and fan the smoke clockwise around the entrance of your home. Say something like this:

> *Great Spirits, (God/Goddess name)*
>
> *I open this humble door,*
>
> *and remove the past left here before.*

4. Enter the home and allow the smoke from the sage to permeate each room. Begin facing North and walk clockwise, fanning the smoke as you go. As you pass a window, open it and allow the energy within the home to move out into the world where it can be dissipated and no longer do harm or affect others again.

Setting the Protection

1. On your altar inside, place the smudge in the small bowl you selected when you were getting ready for this ritual. Extinguish the smudge by dipping it into a little water. The continual energy will be coming from your candles. If you chose to use sandalwood incense, you can allow it to continue to burn; just place it in an incense holder.

2. Start with lighting your protection candle. This is the gold candle you selected in your preparations.

> As before, close your eyes and imagine a flame being lit within your own body.
> Imagine your spiritual essence, lighting a flame in your solar plexus. This is your divine light, the spirit within you that will provide the energy to the wick of your candle.

With each breath you take, imagine the gold flame inside your being
growing stronger and brighter. Until it fills your entire body.

Open your eyes take the matches/lighter in hand and light the
wick of your candle.

As you do, imagine the light within you gaining in strength and
growing yet again, this time your body cannot contain the
energy field and it pushes outside to encompass your physical
being.

Say something like:

Great Spirits, (God/Goddess name)

I bring to light this guardian flame,

sending all fear back from whence it came.

3. With the protection candle lit and ready, you're ready for the Rose
Shield Oil you prepared.

Use your right hand to draw you personal sigil or a pentacle over
the flame. (If you're non-pagan you can draw your religions
primary symbol over the flame. Not too close, you don't want to
get burned.) You can use the center of your palm as the drawing force, the tips of your fingers or just one finger; it's up to
you. I use my middle and ring fingers pressed together, with
my hand open. If you were to look at my hand from above, it
would resemble the hand language sign for "I Love You."

Say something like:

Great Spirits, (God/Goddess name)

I set forth this light of protection

for securing my home and hearth.

Hold the vessel of oil in both hands and present it to the flame
- Say something like:

Great Spirits, (God/Goddess name)

I set forth this protective shield

to guard this home and those who enter

from outside influences this home is sealed.

4. Be careful with your protection potion to ensure you have enough to go around.

Start with the front door and pour a small line of the liquid across its frame on the floor. If you decided to purchase the garland or a few roses, now is the time to hang the garland over the door, or place the roses by the door.

Moving clockwise through each room, do the same thing across the bottom of each windowsill.

As you pass the windows, close them. This is a symbolic gesture locking in your projection.

Setting the Blessing

1. Now you are ready to set your blessing. Back at your altar is your Lavender incense and taper candle. Start with lighting your blessings candle.

As before, close your eyes and imagine a flame being lit within your own body.

Imagine your spiritual essence lighting a flame in your solar plexus. This is your divine light, the spirit within you that will provide the energy to the wick of your candle.

With each breath you take, imagine the Lavender and pink flame inside your being growing stronger and brighter. Until it fills your entire body.

Open your eyes, take the matches/lighter in hand and light the wick of your candle.

As you do, imagine the light within you gaining in strength and growing yet again, this time your body cannot contain the energy field and it pushes outside to encompass your physical being.

Say something like:

Great Spirits, (God/Goddess name)
I bring to light this blessing flame,

{Take your Lavender incense and set it ablaze from the flame of the blessing candle as you speak the final lines of the verse}

to bring forth happiness and joy,
to provide security and abundance,
to share in love, friendship and laughter.

2. Once again moving clockwise through each room, walk the incense through the house.

Combining Your Work

1. Once you have completed each section, you can combine all your work into one area. The best thing to do is move the altar and place it on a fireplace hearth. If your new home does not have a fireplace, you can set the altar under a window in the main living area. The protection candle should be set on the right, the blessing candle on the left. Retrieve your ritual candle from the outside altar and place it in the center. The incense should be placed next to their candle. Everything should be set on the altar in a clockwise manner to maintain the positive energy flow.

Thanking The Great Spirits (God/Goddess)

1. Many people find it appropriate to honor the spirits and deities that they've asked to assist them. I happen to be one of these people. However, for rituals such as this, giving honor through an offering of life, instead of food can also be appropriate. By that I mean, planting a seed or plant in honor of the deities—one that supports or represents the energy of the deity. In this case, a rose bush would be an appropriate offering.

   Raise the unplanted bush and present it to the divine forces. Say something like this:

   I give this offering of rose and thorn as my symbol of gratitude and honor.

   the Great Spirits, whose light and love shall shine through its pedals of beauty, to remind us all of your unselfish gifts.

   Blessings Be To Thee.

Meditation and Closing

1. No matter what your ceremony is for, you should add a moment of meditation to the event. In this altered state, you can add to a spell by visualizing the energy being created, seeing it in your mind as it manifests and comes to form. You can contact the Great Spirits and engage them in a private ritual. You can use this time to thank the forces that have helped you.

2. Here is where you should write a brief summary of the ritual and your experience in your personal *Book of Shadows*. Record any insights you might have gained through the meditation, or any physical feelings, or emotions you might have experienced.

When you have completed this step, face your altar and give thanks once more for this sacred space. Then back away and allow your candles to burn out. Do not leave candles burning unattended. If you can't stay with the altar, its okay to blow out the flames (let them smoke) and re-light them when you return.

~Lady Springwolf

Blowing Away Bad Habits

This spell is for your animal, which may have a bad habit, such as urinating inside the home or scratching on the furniture.

You will need:

1 dandelion that is at its "fluff" stage
White jasmine incense

Go out in your yard or to a neighborhood park to find yourself a dandelion. Pick the dandelion and thank Flora, the Goddess of Nature, for her offering. Be careful not to knock off the fluff. Then find a quiet spot to sit.

Light the incense, hold the flower in front of you, concentrate on the bad habit in your pet that you want to break and repeat the following incantation:

A deep breath in, a strong breath out

This habit (pet's name) can do without

As I blow the fluff into the air

I send with it a healing prayer

May this bad habit be withdrawn

And all memory of it be forever gone

So Mote It Be.

Hold the flower close to your mouth and blow off the fluff. As you watch it scatter and fly away, envision the bad habit flying away with it.

~Marla Brooks
Author, *Animal Spells and Magick*

Morrigan Protection Spell

Morrigan is the Irish Goddess of war, sex, magick, strength, and courage. She is a patroness of witches and of women in particular. She is connected to the land, making her a sovereign goddess. Morrigan offers protection, she teaches one to be strong not meek. Morrigan helps abuse survivors find courage in the face of battle or struggle. She is associated with corvids, Ravens, and crows. Morrigan is also a wonderful Goddess to invoke for people working within the criminal justice system. She protects all who fight for justice—police officers, fire fighters, members of the military, etc. If you cannot find a real crow feather harvested respectfully, a small piece of black marabou feather will suffice from the craft store. This spell should be performed during the Dark of the Moon, her sacred time. Begin first by blending the oil and then perform the ritual.

You will need:

Red candle
Black alter cloth
Raven/Morrigan statue (optional)
Sage bundle
A piece of black tourmaline
Morrigan Oil (*Chant Morrigan's name 9 times while blending*)
Garnet Gemstone Chips
Onyx Gemstone Chips
Quartz Crystal Chips
Pinch of Heather Flowers
Pinch of Mullein
Pinch of Rosemary
Pinch of Dragons Blood
Pinch Red Clover
Pinch Dehydrated Red Apple
Piece of Crow Feather (Harvested respectfully)
6 drops Patchouli Oil
3 drops of Clove Oil
2 Drops Vanilla Oil
2 drops Rose Absolute
Carrier oil-Grape seed

Light the sage bundle to smudge away any negativity in your ritual area. Light the red candle and gaze upon it, let it burn into your third eye. Allow yourself to relax. Gaze now upon the Raven or Morrigan statue. Close your eyes and visualize the great Raven Queen, the Morrigan. Before you she stands, in robes of red, sword in hand, ebony hair, and striking eyes. She motions you with her sword, to rise and fight all that oppresses you.

She then folds her cloak around you, shielding you from harm. Open your eyes,

Take your oil blend and your black tourmaline into your hands and chant the following:

> Morrigan, Morrigan, Morrigan!
>
> Raven Mother, Three x Three!
>
> I ask for your Protection unto me!
>
> That I may find strength where I am weak!
>
> That I may become strong, no longer meek!
>
> I ask for protection and that my will be done
>
> For my highest good and harming none!
>
> So Mote It Be!

Anoint your third eye and the black tourmaline with the Morrigan Oil. Know that you have been blessed by the divine protection of the Dark Raven Goddess.

Continue to wear this oil and carry this stone in honor of Morrigan.

Wear for all situations when you are in need of divine protection, courage, strength, and swift justice.

~Macha Raven Mare

Windy Day Wish Spell

You will need:

One Handful of Flour or Dirt

You need to be standing in a high place either on the porch of an apartment building or even on a stool outside on a windy day. Cup the earth or flower in your right hand and cover it with your left. Visualize your one wish permeating the flour or dirt; see it continue to flow in between your palms – like the earth or flour begins to have a light of its own with the energy you are giving by sending your wish into it. When you feel you have put as much of your vision into the flour or dirt as possible, then say:

Sister Wind, carry my wish so the Goddess may hear my heart's desire.

Release the dirt or flour with a loud yell letting out the rest of the energy that you had been building. After that...forget you ever did it.

One thing I have learned with sympathetic magick is that the more you concentrate on it, the more you doubt it, and the more it backfires. Let it happen; Goddess will provide.

~Lady D.

Money Attraction Spell

Perform this spell during the waxing moon, on a Thursday the day of Jupiter planet of luck or on Sunday ruled by the Sun, planet of success, to bring money to you.

You will need:

Green Candle	Small Green Bag
Small Citrine	Loadstone
Pinch of Pennyroyal	Pine Oil
Blank Check	Green ribbon
Green pen	Acorn
Dollar Bill	Quarter
Nickel	Dime
Penny	

Anoint the green candle with pine oil and light

Write upon the blank check with the green pen the following words:

Money quickly comes to me,

I am prosperous financially,

I have all that I need and even more,

Money now has come to my door

Roll up the blank check, tie up with a green ribbon and place it and all remaining ingredients inside of Muslin bag. Anoint bag with pine oil. Take up the bag into your hands to charge it, repeat the chant aloud three times.

Money quickly comes to me,

I am prosperous financially,

I have all that I need and even more,

Money now has come to my door

For the highest good, and harm to none,

this is my will,

so shall it be done

So Mote It Be!

~ Macha Raven Mare

Banishing Ritual

Before you begin, it is always best to do any kind of spell work within a circle of protection. If you know how to cast a circle then do so. If you do not simply state out loud as you walk in a circle of space where you will perform the ritual:

(3x) I am receptive only to the highest and best influences.

Continue by saying the following:

(1x) May only Love and Light be allowed to enter here, harming none and for the good of all. So Mote It Be!

Get four small pieces of paper and on each piece write the person's name or the name of whatever it is you need to banish. On the opposite side, draw a pentacle. Carve the same word or name and a pentacle on a black candle also. Place your stone to the right of the candle to draw in the magick you are about to perform. Anoint the candle with Banishing Oil and then roll the oiled candle into the Banishing Incense.

Light the charcoal disk in a fireproof container and sprinkle the Ritual Spell Incense Powder onto the disk. (It may take a few moments for the charcoal disk to fully glow and become ember-like. The charcoal is self-igniting as well as the incense so just hold the flame to it until it begins to "sparkle."

Visualize this thing or person drawing away from you and ask your angels, departed loved ones and/or spirit guides for help. Banish! Banish! Banish! By the power of 3x3! Rid yourself and your family of it! End it here and now! Visualize the person, place, or thing going through the motions of truly, once and for all LEAVING. There is no looking back. There is no guilt, fear, or second-guessing. You have cut the "tumor" out of your soul/life. Burn your banishing incense on a hot coal in the proper fireproof container.

Light the candle. Take the four pieces of paper and burn one, saying:

"I banish _____ with the power of fire. So mote it be."

Bury one in some dirt, saying:

"I banish _____ with the power of Earth. So mote it be."

Toss one into any running water, such as a stream; saying:

"I banish _____ with the power of Water. So mote it be."

Then tear one into little pieces and throw it out your window, saying:

"I banish _____ with the power of Wind. So mote it be."

Let your black candle burn down. Visualize the people or things you want banished in your life. Visualize your happiness with them gone from you. Remember, this elated feeling! Breathe easy and let all the tension in your muscles melt away into the ethos.

They are now banished. Carry the stone in your pocket until your spell works and then bury it in the Earth as an offering to the Gods in thanks. You can also keep it to remember the power within you!

*Note: If you prefer to work inside, you can use a toilet flush instead of a stream or brook. It really does not matter how precisely you do this, but it IS important that your intention be clear. It is best also to perform this spell during the Waning Moon or on the Dark of the Moon. Although, if your "need" is great any time will do. The Universe will still hear you.

Always remember:

"**Your words have Strength, your Victory can be Won. Believe as you go, after your Spell is Done! Brightest Blessings!**"

~Rev. Branwyn Willows HPs

"The Love Potion" 1903 by Evelyn de Morgan

Blues Brew

Handed down from John Parkinson since 1640, this wonderful brew helps to raise the spirits when you are feeling down.

Ingredients:

> 2 quarts of apples (cubed)
> 4 quarts water
> 3 Tbsp white vinegar
> 2 Tsp Cinnamon
> 1 Orange cut into small pieces
> 3 Cups Sugar

Directions: Core the apples but do not skin them, then wash the apples in cold water and slice them into one inch cubes. Get your orange and peel the rind, separate the slices and take out the seeds (if necessary). In a large stew pot, mix the water and sugar, bring to boiling for about one minute. Reduce heat and allow to cool slightly. Add apples and cook for approximately three hours stirring often and never allowing the mixture to come to a full boil. Add white vinegar and orange pieces and cinnamon. Allow bring to simmer and keep it there for another 30 minutes stirring frequently. Turn off heat and let mixture cool on the stove. Once cooled, strain the mixture using a doubly ply cheesecloth, squeezing the leftover fruit pieces to remove all the juice.

Pour the liquid into a jug such as a glass cider jug. Let cool until room temperature or place in refrigerator until at desired temperature.

~Lady Springwolf D.D. Ph D.

Spell to Freeze and Bind a Harmful Person

During the Waning Moon or the Dark of the Moon take the following ingredients and assemble.

You will need:

> 1 photo or piece of property or hair from the person doing harm to you
> 1 piece of non-recycled paper or parchment paper
> Black thread, ribbon or tape
> 9 needles, nails, or shards of glass
> 3 pinches of Rosemary, Angelica Root, or Black Cohosh
> 1 black candle
> 1 cup of your own urine
> 1 Mason jar

Light the black candle and go into a spell working state. Black is the color of Protection and will neutralize all from harming you. You may light incense or play music. Concentrate and imagine you are actually binding this person from doing harm. Take the photo and place it in the paper. Begin binding the black thread around it while saying:

I bind you (person's name) from doing all harm, harm to yourself, and harm to others. I bind you (person's name) from doing all harm, harm to yourself, and harm to me. I bind you (person's name) from doing all harm, harm to yourself, and harm to others. As I do will it then, So Mote It Be!

Place the bound piece into the Mason jar. Add the 3 pinches of herb and needles. Add your urine and top it off with purified water. Your urine adds your DNA and essence to the spell, it specifically protect you on a cellular level. Because it is waste, it also strengthens the spell ingredients in the jar to repel all harm. Put the cover on the jar tightly, take the Black candle and seal the jar with the dripping wax. Allow the candle to burn out. Take the jar, place it in a bag, and place it in the back of your freezer; hidden away. You may label it as "Do not touch" if you live with other people.

Before you place it in the freezer draw in the air over it the Banishing Pentagram and state aloud:

I freeze you (person's name) from doing all harm, harm to yourself and harm to others. I freeze you (person's name) from doing all harm, harm to yourself, and harm to me. I freeze you (person's name) from doing all harm, harm to yourself, and harm to others. This spell is fixed, harming none and for the good of all, three times three, as I will it, So Mote It Be!

Bury the spent candle and remaining wax in the ground or throw into the woods.

~ Rev. Branwyn Willows HPs

Full Moon Love Spell

You will need:

> Small red bag with string
> Small round Mirror
> Small white candle
> 3 moonstones
> Rose absolute oil
> Small rose quartz
> Rose buds
> Piece of red cord or string

During a Friday night, which is closest to the full moon; or on the night of the full moon. Find a quiet place outdoors, or in private dark room by a window near moonlight. Place a mirror down, where the moonlight can reflect off it. Anoint a white candle with rose oil; light and place the candle and rose quartz on top of the mirror. Place moonstones around mirror to form the shape of a pyramid. Sprinkle rose buds around the mirror and stones. Take the red string into your hands and focus upon your deepest desires, of what you seek for in a loving partner. Do not use anyone's name or direct it at a specific person, as this interferes with his or her free will. Instead, ask the universe to send to you the person who will be true and correct for you in every way, for the highest good and harming none. When you have focused your intentions and your desires, chant this rhyme three times:

> Lovely lady of the moon
> Grant to me this heart wish boon
> That unto me will come a love
> As gentle and sweet as the dove
> Be it only the most perfect and correct
> partner for me.
> This is heartfelt wish
> So Mote It Be

Then tie three knots in the string and chant:

By knot of one, the spell is done
By knot of two, my wish has come true
By knot of three, So Mote it be
For the highest good for all involved, harming none, in the
lady's name, the spell is done!

Reflect upon your wish as if it has already come true, and it will. Let the candle burn out on its own, when it is finished tie up the mirror, stones, roses, rose quartz and knotted cord into the red bag. Keep this bag under your pillow at night while you sleep and leave undisturbed as you dream of your new love.

Know the energy of the full moon is still at work, as it has been charging within the mirror. On the next Full moon, unite one knot in the string and replace the bag under your pillow; repeating your chant to the moon goddess. You will repeat this for the next two full moons until all of your knots have been untied and all of the magick is finally released. Your heart's desire should have reached fruition before or near the third full moon.

~Macha Raven Mare

My Daily Devotionals

Sunrise

"O' Anu, Mother of Dawn
Help me on this bright new morn.
Aid me with your power
And strengthen it every hour."

Morning

"O' Danu, Mother of the Gods
Goddess of wells, magick, plenty & wisdom.
Protect your daughter throughout this day
Come to me at length and stay."

Noon

"Great Gaia, Abundant Mother
Fair & Bright!
Bless me during the mid-day light
Be with me now and 'til the moonlight."

Afternoon

"Goddess Mother, the day, it wanes
Hearken & hear me as I call your name!
Take me now, where I must go
And to me, my destiny show."

Sunset

"Setting Sun of passing day
Aid me in your gentle way.
Take my spell O' Ancient One
And give it your strength
As the day is done."

Evening

"O' Selene, Magickal Moon Goddess
Maiden Bright!
Hear me now, Hearken to me this night
Aid my spells in taking flight!
To it's target, now please guide.
Increase it's power as it flies!"

~Rev. Branwyn Willows *HPs*

Contributor Biographies

I have included the bio's of the witches, wiccans, and pagans that so wonderfully allowed me to share their works with the readers. You are all such beautiful individuals and it is an honor to call each of you my friend and my sister.

Marla Brooks

Marla Brooks lives in Hollywood, California, is an author of the *Ghosts of Hollywood* series of books as well as her new books Workplace Spells and *Animal Spells and Magick*. Marla Brooks is a talk show host on the Para-X Radio network and CBS Radio with her highly successful show "Stirring the Cauldron." Marla Brooks has been a celebrity writer and practicing witch for many years.

Lady D.

Hailing from mystical New England, **Lady D.** has traveled extensively in her search for knowledge within the Craft. She is a practicing High Priestess in the Frost Tradition and first learned of the Craft through her mother's own pursuits in spirituality. Most of the rituals and spells that Lady D. works with are from within her coven and family. Lady D. especially loves working with Elemental Energies, including in the realms of faeries and other wonderful creatures. Her particular favorite element to work with is wind, and she finds this to be one of the easiest to work with.

Macha Raven Mare

Macha Raven Mare lives in New Hampshire. She is a Pagan, Witch, and a Priestess of the Old Religion. She has been walking the path of the witch for over sixteen years. Like most new comers to the path, Macha Raven did not have access to a teacher or coven family. Knowing only very few people within a small rural pagan community, she sought out on her own, diving into every book she could find on the subject. Macha studied all she could on the subject of Paganism, Wicca and Witchcraft, taking inspiration, from such leaders like Scott Cunningham, Raven Grimassi, Laurie Cabot, Chris Penczak. She then set out, formed, and facilitated a study group called Ravens Grove Mother, a community and friendship, for people like herself; who sought out to make connections to share their love and passion for the Craft together.

Rev. Branwyn Willows HPs

Rev. Branwyn Willows is a Celtic High Priestess and native of Enchanted New England. She has been a witch all her life and has a passion to share the Goddess's love, healing, and magick with others. A side from being a High Priestess in the craft, Branwyn is also a Psychic Medium who has been reading professionally for the past five years. Rev. Branwyn does not condone the use of baneful magick, as she believes in Karmic Law, the Threefold Law, in that what you put out comes back to you threefold whether in this life or the next. As a witch, High Priestess and psychic medium, she believes that she is here to help and heal people. All magick is pre-formed with Love and Light, harming none and for the good of all. She is an ordained Minister of the Universal Life Church with a Master of Wiccan Studies degree. In addition, she legally performs all Wiccan/Pagan Rites of Passage in her local area including, but not limited to, Handfastings, Wiccanings, and Funeral Rites.

Lady SpringWolf D.D. Ph.D

Director of Pagan's Path, owner and President of Spring's Haven, LLC., **Lady SpringWolf** has been studying spiritual and metaphysical principles for almost 30 years. She is an ordained Metaphysical Minister of the International Metaphysical Ministry, a 50-year-old organization of Metaphysical practitioners and education. She holds a Doctorate of Divinity in Metaphysical Science and a Doctor of Philosophy in Pastoral Counseling Psychology from the University of Sedona and is a member of the American Metaphysical Doctors Association. Through informal and formal study, she has acquired various certificates, certifications, degrees, and licenses from her spiritual path, through esoteric schools, holistic training programs and formal collegiate institutions.

A Final Word

As I've said throughout this book, I think that in order to move forward in the future, we must first look at the past. That being said, I feel our focus should always be on the future. Every day I am seeing new Gerald Gardners, Doreen Valientes, and Laurie Cabots coming into the fold and raising their voices.

Each of these leaders began on their own, each walked for sometime a solitary path; most witches begin this way. Most fell into a role of leadership, managing both the responsibilities the best they knew how. But each was not afraid to let their hearts speak, each was not afraid to answer the call of the Goddess when She asked them to stand up for Her and the freedom of Her children. No matter what you are—pagan, wiccan, witch—do not be afraid to raise your voice; remember you are not alone and that your voice counts.

Be Proud. Be Heard.
Katie Boyd

Ancestor worship is an integral part of most witchcraft or pagan traditions. Here we honor our loved ones during a Samhain ritual.

Resources

Here are some really great sites and information which will help one in the journey for knowledge and learning about the Craft.

Shops

Laurie Cabot's Shop
The Cat, The Crow and The Crown
63R Wharf Street
Salem, Massachusetts 01970
(978) 744-6274
LaurieCabot.com

White Light Pentacles/Sacred Spirit Products
176 Federal Street
Salem, Massachusetts 01970
www.wlpssp.com

Misty Meadows Farm and Herbal Center
183 Wednesday Hill Road
Lee, New Hampshire 03861
(603)-659-7211
www.mistymeadows.org

Schools

The Church and School of Wicca
Gavin and Yvonne Frost
PO Box 297-IN
Hinton, West Virginia 25951-0297 USA
www.wicca.org

Witch School
Great place to learn online or in person
www.witchschool.ws/main.asp

Campus in:
Rossville, Illinois
117 S. Chicago St.
Rossville, Illinois 60963

Life Force Arts Center
3148 N. Lincoln
Chicago, Illinois 60654

Network sites

www.cog.org
http://groups.yahoo.com/group/RavensGroveCircle
www.witchvox.com
www.witches.meetup.com

Witch/Wicca Information sites

www.ClanofTubalCain.org.uk
www.doreenvaliente.com
www.geraldgardner.com
www.lotuspond.silentblue.net
www.lwhps.tripod.com
www.Thepaganspath.com

Witchcraft History Sites

The Museum of Witchcraft,
Boscastle
Cornwall PL35 0HD
01840 250111
www.museumofwitchcraft.com
www.Controverscial.com
http://digital.library.cornell.edu/w/witch/index.html
www.sacred-texts.com
wwww.thewica.co.uk

Activist and Civil Rights Organizations

Project Witches' Protection
203 Washington Street Suite 225
Salem Massachusetts 01870
(978)-666-0758
www.witchesprotection.com

The Glass Temple
www.glasstemple.com
www.us.paganfederation.org
www.milpagan.org

Radio Show Sites

ISIS Paranormal Radio
http://www.isisinvestigations.com/
Don't be fooled! They cover everything
Wicca, Witchcraft and Esoteric too!

Stirring the Cauldron
www.para-x.com/stirringthecauldron.com
www.stirringthecauldron.podomatic.com
www.stirringthecauldron.planetparanormal.com

Magazines

www.circlesanctuary.org
www.fullmoonrisingmagazine.com
www.newwitch.com
www.mysteriesmagazine.com
www.sagewoman.com
www.spellcraft.com
www.thewitchesalmanac.com

Aradia

or the

Gospel of the

Witches

by

Charles G. Leland,

London

David Nutt,

270-71 Strand,

1899

Books of the Elders

Sybil Leek's Books

A Shop in the High Street (ca. 1962, '64, '65)
Have Mania, Will Collect (1964)
A Fool and a Tree (1964)
Mr. Hotfoot Jackson (1965)
The Jackdaw and the Witch: A True Fable (1966)
Diary of a Witch (1968)
The Astrological Cookbook (1968)
Sybil Leek's Astrological Guide to Love and Sex (1969)
Numerology: The Magic of Numbers (1969)
Sybil Leek's Book of Fortune Telling (1969)
The Tree that Conquered the World (1969)
Cast Your Own Spell (ca. 1970, '72, '75)
How to Be Your Own Astrologer (1970)
Phrenology (1970)
Sybil Leek's Astrological Guide to Successful Everday Living (1970)
The Complete Art of Witchcraft (ca. 1971 or '73)
Telepathy: The Respectable Phenomenon (1971)
ESP: The Magic Within You (1971)
My Life in Astrology (1972)
The Astrological Guide to Financial Success (1972)
The Astrological Guide to the Presidential Candidates (1972)
The Bicycle: That Curious Invention (1973)
The Story of Faith Healing (1973)
Sybil Leek's Book of Herbs (1973, '80)
How to Succeed through Astrology (1973)
The Best of Sybil Leek (1974)
Reincarnation: The Second Chance (1974)
Sybil Leek's Zodiac of Love (1974)
Tomorrow's Headlines Today (1974)
Sybil Leek's Book of Curses (1975)
Driving Out the Devils (1975)
Herbs: Medicine & Mysticism (1975)
The Night Voyagers: You and Your Dreams (1975)
Star Speak: Your Body Language from the Stars (1975)
Dreams (1976)
Sybil Leek on Exorcism: Driving Out the Devils (1976)
The Assassination Chain (1976)

Inside Bellevue (1976)
A Ring of Magic Islands (1976)
Sybil Leek's Book of the Curious and the Occult (1976)
Moon Signs (1977)
Astrology and Love (1983)

Laurie Cabot's Books

Power of the Witch: The Earth, the Moon, and the Magical Path to Enlightenment
(1990)
Love Magic (1992)
Celebrate the Earth: A Year of Holidays in the Pagan Tradition (1994)
*The Witch in Every Woman: Reawakening the Magical Nature of the Feminine to
Heal, Protect, Create, and Empower* (1997)

Doreen Valiente's Books

Witchcraft for Tomorrow (1993)
An ABC of Witchcraft Past and Present (1994)
Natural Magic (1999)
Witchcraft: A Tradition Renewed (1999)
Charge of the Goddess: The Mother of Modern Witchcraft (2000)
The Rebirth of Witchcraft (2008)

Gerald Gardner's Books

High Magic's Aid, (1949, self-published)
High Magic's Aid: Wonderful Tale of Medieval Witchcraft (1999)
Gardner's Book of Shadows (2000)
Witchcraft Today (2004)
The Meaning of Witchcraft (2008)

Alex and Maxine Sanders Books

Maxine: The Witch Queen (1976)
Alex Sanders Lectures (1984)
Fire Child: The life & Magic of Maxine Sanders "Witch Queen" (2007)

Gavin Frost's Books

*The Magic Power of Witchcraft (Ellis Horwood Series in Polymer Science and
Technology)* (1976)
Meta-Psychometry: Key to Power and Abundance (1978)
Modern witch's guide to beauty, vigor, and vitality (1978)
A Witch's Guide To Life (1978)

Astral Travel: Your Guide to the Secrets of Out-Of-The-Body Experiences (1985)
Tantric Yoga: The Royal Path to Raising Kundalini Power (1989)
The Prophet's Bible (1991)
Tantric Yoga: The Royal Path to Raising Kundalini Power (1996)
The Magic Power of White Witchcraft: Revised for the Millenium (1999)
Good Witch's Bible (1999)
A Witch's Grimoire of Ancient Omens. Portents, Talismans, Amulets, & Charms (1999)
Power Secrets from a Sorcerer's Private Magnum Arcanum (1999)
Power Secrets From a Sorcerer's Private Magnum Arcana (1999)
The Witch's Magical Handbook (2000)
Witch's Grimoire of Ancient Omens, Portents, Talismans, Amulets, and Cha (2002)
The Witch's Book of Magical Ritual: Use the Forces of Wicca to Direct Your Psychic Powers (2002)
Witch's Grimoire 6-Copy Counter Display (2002)
A Witch's Guide to Psychic Healing: Applying Traditional Therapies, Rituals, and Systems (2003)
The Solitary Wiccan's Bible (2004)
Good Witches Fly Smoothly: Surviving Witchcraft (2006)
The Bible of Sex Magic and Enlightenment (2007)
A Modern Grail Quest (2007)
The Dancing Detective: Two Books in One (2008)

Books of the Modern Witch

Today's modern witch has many resources at their fingertips—one of which is reading, another the internet and so forth. Here I have decided to include some of my personal favorite titles from modern witches.

Hexcraft by Silver Ravenwolf
Solitary Wicca by Scott Cunningham
Grimoire for the Green Witch by Ann Moura
Witchcraft Theory and Practice by Ly de Angeles
Kitchen Witches Cookbook by Patricia Telesco
Coven Craft: Witchcraft for Three or More by Amber K
Italian Witchcraft: The Old Religion of Southern Europe by Raven Grimassi
If You Want To Be A Witch: A Practical Introduction to The Craft by Edain McCoy
Charms, Spells and Formulas by Ray T. Marlborough
Hedge Witch: Guide to Solitary Witchcraft by Rae Beth
Workplace Spells: Everyday Magick on the Job by Marla Brooks
Circle, Coven and Grove by Deborah Blake
The Craft: A Witch's Book of Shadows by Dorothy Morrison

Bibliography

Origins of Witchcraft

Admin. "I Want Pagan Holidays." *Pentacle* Magazine (on-line), 05 December 2003.

Carrell, Severin. "Campaign to pardon the last witch, jailed as a threat to Britain at war: Salem experts support appeal to overturn 'ludicrous' conviction" Guardian.co.uk. Jan 13, 2007.

Essex County Archives, Salem. "Answer for Mary Bradbury." Witchcraft Vol. 2 p.35.

Essex County Archives, Salem. "Indictment v Mary Bradbury No. 2." Witchcraft Vol. 2 p.34-37.

Essex County Archives. Salem. "James Kettle v. Sarah Bishop." Witchcraft Vol. 2 p.55.

Essex County Archives. Salem. "Section: Thomas Bradbury for Mary Bradbury." Witchcraft Vol. 2 p.36.

Essex County Archives. Salem. "Section: Samuel Endicott v. Mary Bradbury." Witchcraft Vol. 2 p. 37.

"Fly By Night, The Autobiography of Zsuzsanna Budapest on disk The Early Years." Published by the Women's Spirituality Forum in 2008.

Gibbons, Jenny. "Recent developments in the study of the great European Witch hunt." at: http://www.cog.org/witch_hunt.html.

Greer, Jeremiah. "India Witch Trials." *Mysteries* Magazine Issue 24, Fall 2009. Pg 6.

Hutton, Ronald. "Triump of the Moon: A History of Modern Pagan Witchcraft." Oxford University Press (1999).

Padzer, Lawrence, & Michelle Smith. *Michelle Remembers*, Pocket Books, (1980).

Scott, Sir Walter, ed. Brinsley Nicholson M.D. "Discoverie of Witchcraft." Elliot Stock 52 Patterson Row E.C. pg 89 (1886).

Shlacter, Barry. "Bothered and Bewildered; Wiccans at Hood Shrug Off Media," *Star-Telegram* (8/7/99).

Shlachter, Barry. "Bothered and bewildered; Wiccans at Hood shrug off media hubbub." *Fort Worth Star Telegram*, 1999-AUG-7.

Slattery, Elisa. "'To Prevent a 'Shipwreck of Souls': Johann Weyer and 'De Praestigiis Daemonum'," published in "Essays in History," by the Corcoran Department of History, University of Virginia, Volume 36, (1994), Page 76.

Spaeth, Adolph, and L.D. Reed, Henry Eyster Jacobs, et Al., Trans. & Eds. *Works of Martin Luther*,

(Philadelphia: A. J. Holman Company, 1915), Vol.1, pp. 29-38.

Stephen Hayes, "Christian responses to Witchcraft and sorcery," at: http://hayes-fam.bravehost.com/witch1.htm.

Stephens, Walter. "Demon lovers: Witchcraft, Sex and Belief," University of Chicago, (2000).

"Teaching Assistant Claims, She was Sacked for Being a Witch." *The Argus*, March 20, 2007.

"Why are there Witches? History of Witchcraft for Halloween," News release, Johns Hopkins University Office of News and Information, 1999-OCT-11.

Wiccan Pagan Witch What?

O'Donnell, James J. "*PAGANUS*," Classical Folia 31(1977) 163-69. Online at: http://ccat.sas.upenn.edu/

Mohrmann, C. "*Encore une fois: paganus*," 'tudes sur le latin des chr'tiens (Rome, 1958-1965), 3.277-289; orig. pub. in Vigiliae Christianae, 6 (1952), 109-121. Quoted in Ref. 16.

Sybil Leek

My Life in Astrology, Published by Prentice-Hall; First Edition, 1972.

Sybil Leek's Book of Fortune Telling. New York: Collier, 1969.

Gerald Gardner

Witchcraft Today. Published by Rider & Company, 1954.

Alexander Sanders

Cavendish, R., A., C., & Innes, B. (1994). *Man, Myth and Magic*. London: Marshall Cavendish.

Duffy, David. "Amazing Black Magic Rites on Cheshire Hillside." *Manchester Evening Chronicle*, 15 Sept. 1962: 2.

Hutton, Ronald. *The Triumph of the Moon*. Oxford Oxfordshire: Oxford University Press, 2001.

Johns, June (1969). *King of the Witches*. New York: Coward-McCann, Inc.

Tyson, James. "The *Men Only* Interview: Alex Sanders." *Men Only* magazine, Paul Raymond Publications, UK, 1973: 39-41,74.

The Witchcrafting Podcast by Karagan, Portugal, 21 August 2007.

Doreen Valiente

Knowles, George. "Robert Cochrane" 23, March 2003. Controverscial.com 14, Nov. 2009. http://www.controverscial.com/Robert%20Cochrane.htm.

Semple, Gavin W. "A Poisoned Chalice: The Death of Robert Cochrane" Reineke Verlaig, 2004 pp 6-12.

Valiente, Doreen. "LETTER OF WELCOME FROM DOREEN VALIENTE" *Pentagram* Vol 1 Issue 1, August 1964 pp 1.
Valiente, Doreen, "Why the Monomark?" *Pentagram*, Vol 1 Issue 1, August 1964.

Laurie Cabot

Laurie Cabot, *Power of the Witch*, published by Delta; Later Printing edition, 1990.

Covens

Gardner, Gerald. *The Meaning of Witchcraft*. published by Magickal Childe 1988.
Leek, Sybil. *Diary of a Witch*. published by Fewin, 1975.

Magick of the Elders

Cabot, Laurie. *Power of the Witch*. Published by Delta; Later Printing edition, 1990, pp.222-223.
Cabot, Laurie.*The Magic Door Presents: A Salem Witch's Herbal Magic*. Celtic Crow Publishing, 1994.
Gardnerian Book of Shadows,The Witches' Chant. 1957.
Shakespeare, William. *Macbeth: IV.* The Random House Book of Poetry for Children.1983, pp.10-19; 35-38.
Leek, Sybil. *The Complete Art of Witchcraft.*" N.Y. : Signet, 1973, 8th Printing